THE CHRISTIAN NEUROSIS

PIERRE SOLIGNAC

The Christian Neurosis

CROSSROAD · NEW YORK

1982
The Crossroad Publishing Company
575 Lexington Avenue, New York, NY 10022

Copyright © 1976 by Éditions de Trévise

Translation © John Bowden 1982

Printed in the United States of America

Library of Congress Catalog Card No.: 81-72066

ISBN 0-8245-0108-X

CONTENTS

PREFACE

Neurosis is a psychogenic state, the symptoms of which are the symbolic expression of a psychological conflict. This conflict stems from an attempt to compromise between desire and defence, and its roots are to be found in the childhood history of the subject.

After twenty years of medical practice, during which I have tried to concentrate on personal medicine, I have been struck by the fact that traditional Christian education encourages neurotic troubles and the psychosomatic ailments which they produce.

A number of factors have forced me to reflect on the question why so many of the people who come to see me suffer from organic troubles which are simply an expression of their personal anxiety and the difficulties they find in living. These factors include my Christian education; my medical and psychiatric studies; and the fact that I have treated many priests, religious, and 'involved laity'.

More and more priests are leaving the priesthood; the seminaries are emptying and no new novices are coming along; yet more than ever young people are looking for God and for a meaning in life.

Does Christian education allow people to develop and respond to the revolutionary message of Christ: 'Love one another as I have loved you'?

PART I

THE CHRISTIAN NEUROSIS
AND THE INDIVIDUAL

1

The Sanctification of Oppression

Of his own accord, one of my patients who suffered from an anxiety neurosis brought me his Catholic family notebook, given to him on his marriage in 1939. On the last page, in large letters, had been written the following text:

You are a Christian.
Remember that today you must
serve and glorify your God,
imitate Jesus your saviour,
pray to the Virgin his mother,
atone for your sins,
save your soul,
perhaps even suffer death,
escape hell,
attain heaven.

The following prayer must be recited to obtain plenary indulgence at the point of death: 'O Lord my God, from henceforth I accept from your hand death and all its anguish, pain and sorrow, no matter what form it may take, with a tranquil and submissive heart, in accordance with your will.' (Anyone who recites this prayer in either Latin or French, having confessed their sins and received holy communion, even if that should be in full health and long before their death, will obtain plenary indulgence which will be accorded to them at the moment of death, provided that they die with a pure conscience.)

A fine figure of a priest

A priest about fifty years old came to consult me because he was suffering from headaches, spells of dizziness, pains in the stomach and pelvis, and vomiting. His symptoms had resisted all treatment for a period of ten years. He continued to function as a parish priest, as best he could. He went from one specialist to another, being particularly concerned to consult ear, nose and throat specialists, and specialists in gastro-enterology. His medical notes were enormous: a great many blood tests, electro-cardiograms, and X-rays of the head, bladder and intestine.

Our first conversation was devoted to the long story of the symptoms of his illness. He described to me in detail the colour, smell and solidity (or otherwise) of his stools, the intensity of his dizzy spells (which were particularly troublesome when he said mass or gave communion), and the length of his insomnia, caused by stabbing pains in the pelvis which compelled him to get up several times a night to pass water.

After giving him a careful clinical examination, I looked at all his other examinations, one by one. The most recent one had been made only a few weeks previously. Once again, it was completely normal. As often happens in my regular practice, I had to tell him that there was nothing organically wrong with him and that physically he was completely sound. However, I was well aware that he was sick; that he was suffering and in need of treatment, not just medical, but also psychological.

The fact that I had taken him seriously and that I accepted him as a sick man seemed to relieve him. I prescribed very simple treatment for him and asked him to come back, if he was prepared to, so that we could talk at greater length about himself, his life as a priest, his difficulties, and his problems past and present. 'The troubles of which you complain,' I said, 'can only be understood if we go one step beyond considering them as isolated problems, external to your personality. We need to put them in context, in your past and present history.'

Although he did not really understand what I was telling him, this priest agreed to come back and talk about something other than his illnesses.

The first consultations which followed were rather difficult, because my patient found it hard to talk about himself. He kept beginning by telling me in detail all the troubles he had had since our last encounter. Then, little by little, he began to become interested in his personal story, and he passed this on to me, bit by bit. The sixth consultation was an important turning point in our relationship: he did not talk about his troubles in any way. What follows is a very brief summary of what he told me.

'When I think about my childhood, I am struck by the fact that I have so few memories of my father. My mother's marriage took her a long way from the region where she was born. She felt out of place, and her only real contacts were with her parish priest. I feel certain that at a very early stage she decided that her only son should become a priest. She wrapped me in cotton wool and set me aside to make this sacrifice. My education was based on fear, a sense of duty and a feeling of importance. I was often reminded of the saying of General Lapérine, "When we have to choose between two courses, we must always take the harder: fear is the sign of duty." Very soon I had nightmares; I saw myself burning in the fires of hell; I seemed to be crying out like a lost soul. The doctor reassured my mother, telling her that this was adolescent feverishness. In fact, the whole of my childhood was haunted by the thought of mortal sin, and I went to confession often because I was afraid that I had not accused myself sufficiently. I can remember a text from my catechism. It was entitled: "I deserve hell for my sins." I read it and re-read it so often that I still know it almost off by heart:
"Terrible are the tortures of the damned in hell. They are deprived, for ever, of the sight of God. They suffer in a fire a thousand times hotter than fires on earth. Ceaselessly they hear blasphemies, cries of rage and despair. They are in the world of demons. And how long will this fearful torture go on? It will last for ever, for eternity. Hell is a terrible place, and that is where a mortal sin brings us. Perhaps at this very moment I may have mortal sins in my heart. So if I were to die now, I would be cast down into hell. O God, do not let me die in that state! I sincerely repent of all my sins and promise never to offend you again."
My mother refrained from any sign of tenderness towards me; I had to be hardened. She would kiss me on the forehead and then hold out her right cheek to me. I cannot remember ever her having taken me on her knees. Once she took me in her arms: the day of my first communion. At the end of the lunch, the parish priest announced that I would be entering a seminary, because I had a vocation. Jesus had told me in my heart that I should be a priest. I was stupified and disturbed; Jesus had not told me anything of the kind. However, the delight of those present, the smile and the

tenderness of my mother, the fact of being a star who had the right to the first piece of the cake, to some extent allayed my disquiet and my doubts.

And so I entered the minor seminary. My first impressions were not pleasant ones. It was an enormous, melancholy building built in Napoleonic style, with long dark corridors and enormous dormitories. To think of the times I passed along them, in a silent procession, hands behind my back, under the severe eye of a priest who was watching for the slightest whisper. We were watched over with the utmost severity, and the besetting fear of all our teachers was that we would have special friendships. In the playground, we had to play all together. If one of us stayed quietly in a corner or wanted to play by himself, he was immediately accused of having evil thoughts. For two people to be together by themselves was an even more serious matter. It was impossible to have a friend, because any privileged relationship was thought to be unhealthy. In the dormitory we had to sleep with both hands on the counterpane. . .

I can remember one of my first confessions. I could not understand the questions the priest asked me. "Do you have evil thoughts?" There was a questioning silence on my part. "Do you let your mind wander?" "Yes, that happens. I dream of what I would have liked to do. I'm very fond of odd jobs. I would have liked to be a joiner." "Do you touch yourself?" "Touch what?" After a silence, which seemed to me to be full of menace, the priest sent me off with two "Hail Mary's" for penance.

Throughout this period I worked very hard. I was top of the form. That gave me a certain status with my fellow pupils and my teachers. When I went home I had the impression of being someone apart. My mother kissed me on the forehead, and my father shook my hand. I never knew whether he approved of my vocation. He never told me what he thought. While I was at home the parish priest would come to visit us regularly. He was very interested in my being top, and congratulated me, tweaking my ear as he did so.

I have memories of a solitary childhood; no friends at the minor seminary, and no friends at home. I watched longingly while neighbouring children fought, ran about and shouted in the next-door garden. My dignity as a seminarian did not allow me to engage in such revels. I went for long walks by myself in the country. Sometimes my father went with me. He did not say anything, and held my hand tightly. With the end of his walking-stick he would point out various flowers and shrubs to me, telling me their Latin names. We never had a single conversation.

When my cousins came home, I felt that they were both embarrassed and admiring at the same time. We would sit quietly in the drawing room, listening to the talk of the grown-ups. From time to time we were allowed to play dominoes or beggar-my-neighbour. I made it a point of honour to win all the games. That was in fact my only means of expressing my aggressiveness.

I found the summer holidays a particularly painful trial. Every morning I would go to serve at mass at seven o'clock, and then I would help the sacristan to arrange the ornaments. He was a retired old soldier. He and my father were perhaps the only ones to have perceived my sadness and perplexity. After mass, he would often take me home with him to show me some trophy that he had brought back from his campaigns. In particular, he had a splendid sabre which he said had cut off several heads. I remember dreaming about it. I would see myself in the playground of the minor seminary, cutting off the heads of my fellow-pupils; never, I think, those of my teachers.

On Sundays I would take the collection at all the masses. At the end of the service, the parish priest would cast an appraising eye on the contents of the basket. He often showed his discontent: "They are always so mean; I will tell them next Sunday."

The collections were always larger when a missionary came to preach in aid of missions, seminaries or elderly priests. The size of the collection was directly proportional to the vehemence and loquacity of the preacher.

I amused myself by working out which were the most profitable arguments (I worked out their profitability by the number of notes in the collection). Charity and love of one's unfortunate neighbours had the least impact. The accumulation of material goods, a sign of baseness and selfishness, which infringed Christ's poverty, had hardly greater success.

In fact, guilt and fear proved to be most profitable. I remember a missionary, powerful and sunburnt, who had the gift of filling my basket right to the brim. He always used the same kind of arguments: "Your attachment to money will be your downfall, and you will end up in hell. Are you sure that you have acquired it honestly, and have not exploited your neighbours? I am sure that some of you must have bad consciences. Share your goods so that you obtain the indulgence of the Lord."

All these statements left me feeling vaguely disturbed. This appeal to a bad conscience troubled me. I felt the approach was fake, without being able to work out why. I have always had guilt feelings about money, and I think that these childhood Sunday diatribes have something to do with it.

Going to major seminary was a real liberation for me. Each of us had a room of our own, and we could read late into the evening without being bothered. We were not allowed to go into one another's rooms; our territory was really our own. The official reason was that we did not have time to waste in sterile discussions. We could meet in the refectory or during recreation periods.

What stay with me from my education in the major seminary are slogans based on ideas of importance, duty and obedience. It was at this time that I had my first anxieties and my first insomnia. I lived in fear of never having done enough. I always felt guilty about something. My first masturbation goes back to this period. Each time I was left with gnawing anxiety. I would immediately go to my spiritual director, who as a penance would give me some pages of St Augustine, St Thérèse or the gospels to read. He would have done better to advise me to go for long walks, followed by a cold shower.

Having been brought up in an atmosphere of obsessive fear of homosexuality and particular friendships, I discovered the equally obsessive fear of women, the symbols of every vice and every danger.

When we went out, which was always as a group, I tried never to look at a woman. I attempted to keep my gaze neither too high nor too low. Our sexual education was virtually nil. It was limited to a series of prohibitions: never receive an unaccompanied woman in the study, but see her only at the confessional; be very strict about women's dress in church, prohibiting excessively short skirts, or trousers. Seeing a woman's body was the origin of evil thoughts. It was only much later that I discovered that life is inevitably sexual, and that psychologically an emotional relationship with a woman is vital for our equilibrium. This was the time when I made my first friendship. I had had to wait until I was twenty-two to discover all its richness. We were always together, and quickly became suspect. The Superior interviewed us separately, to submit us to a long and formal interrogation. He questioned me for a long time about the character of our relationship, and spoke to me of the dangers of too exclusive a relationship with one of my fellow-students. He asked whether I had sexual problems, whether I masturbated or had bad dreams. I left his room bewildered and anxiety-stricken. Fortunately, my friend was more conversant with sexual problems than I was. He explained himself clearly to the Superior and dared to pronounce the work homosexuality in front of him. He reassured the Superior, affirming the purity of our relations and telling him of his desire, if he ever left the seminary, to marry and have lots of children.

He reported this conversation to me with great amusement, and told me how stupefied the Superior was when told of his student's possible offspring. This was a salutary development, because the Superior, perhaps somewhat disturbed at the thought of the premature departure of a heterosexual seminarian, left us alone for the rest of the academic year.

What else shall I tell you about my life at the major seminary? There was the feeling of not having been prepared for modern life. The theology which I was taught seemed to be the parroting of a system in which everything was dead. One of our superiors was fond of repeating, "As to the emotional life of the priest, I have three things to tell you about what it might be: first, nothing; second, nothing; third, nothing." There followed a brief silence, while he enjoyed the effect he had had. I accepted the priesthood with a good conscience, taking into consideration the relativity of it all. I'm the kind of wood from which people make flutes. Having finally committed myself, I said to myself, "In the end, it doesn't make all that difference whether one marries or becomes a priest, so let's get on with it." When I come to think of it, I believe that my mother's wishes had a great influence on me. It's not for nothing that there are associations for the mothers of priests, and no associations for fathers of priests or even just parents of priests. My father died of a cerebral haemorrhage during my first year at major seminary. I think that the poor man died of never being able to express himself. My mother had become increasingly hard, and she was the image of the model Christian, spending her whole life either at church or in good works. I now wonder what kind of emotional or sex life my father had. Probably none at all. I'm certain that if we had had a real relationship, my life would have changed fundamentally. The only man to have a say at home was the parish priest. Throughout this whole business his role seems to me to have been very ambiguous. . . The image of the dictator, he would just pontificate. . . Poor father!

When I began life as a priest, I felt full of humility and imperfections. I often repeated to myself that saying of Péguy's, "It is for everyone to struggle as best he can; God will decide." Little by little, I built up a prestigious image as a priest, full of interior castles after the fashion of St Teresa. I could have faced any monster, because I had a breastplate made of a sense of importance, honesty and a sense of duty. I was appointed curate in one of the best parishes in the diocese (one like Saint-Séverin used to be, twenty years ago). In this setting my personage could function in a quite brilliant way. It was at that time that a woman in a bus, on sight of me, exclaimed, "What a fine figure of a priest!"

I developed, completely at my ease, in a middle-class world which understood my language. In my sermons, I used with panache all the knowledge I had acquired: the spirituality of fear, of anxiety and of prohibition. I was respected; I even had the impression of being on a pedestal. When I think back to that period, though, it seems that I was not completely comfortable. I was exalted in every respect. I was playing a role which was apparently coherent, but which my self-criticism disclaimed. I gave my parishioners the same education as that which I had received. I judged, I affirmed, I condemned, without ever listening. I think that I was giving vent to my aggression. After several years of this life, which apparently posed no problems, I was offered several posts which would have interested anyone intent on making a career. I refused them. I asked for the poorest parish in the diocese, a parish in the industrial suburbs, particularly run down and completely on the periphery of the society which I knew. The people there were human wrecks, withdrawn into an opposition to everything that has meaning in life: dignity, trust, friendship, freedom, tenderness, happiness. This opposition was particularly crystallized against the church, the symbol of the powers of exploitation, oppression and contempt which had prevailed there at other times. The absence of all the human values which I have mentioned brought about an almost complete inability to communicate, a kind of blockage consisting in a refusal to find any way out. There my drama began. I arrived in this parish, full of passion and enthusiasm, with my fine priestly image of the priest. In a few months I had emptied my church of the few parishioners who still came. The middle-class parishioners were afraid of my aggressiveness, which expressed itself in social concern; the exploiters turned tail and ran. Those who were being exploited didn't understand a word I said. Today's church wants to court the worker, in the same way as it once courted the middle class, but the worker, above all the worker who lives in a ghetto, drawn in on his unhappiness, as was the case with that very poor parish, is not in a position to understand the traditional language of the church, even if we have the impression of bringing it to his doorstep. I believe that in that parish people did not have a vocabulary of more than three hundred words. Communication did not exist. They knew nothing of tenderness or friendship, and they lived shut up in their little family cells. Ignored by everyone, I experienced immense isolation there. My inner world was shattered. That is the time when all my troubles began. I turned in on myself. Solely preoccupied with my physical symptoms, I suppressed my aggression and my anxiety. Speaking with you, I now understand the meaning of regression in an illness. I had no other solution. My "organic ailments" prevented me from foundering in depression and despair.

I now realize how oppressive my education was. The recruiting priest of my childhood was never interested in me. He needed vocations, for the greater glory of God and for his own glory. Not one of my teachers or my spiritual directors tried to discover the reasons for my vocation. I was a good pupil who did not present any problems. I did not once question myself. I can sum up my education in a sentence: "To be at the service of one's neighbour, to obliterate oneself before him and to exist only through him."

But how can you communicate with someone else when you are incapable of communicating with yourself? How can you love someone else when you are incapable of loving yourself? I feel guilty all the time. I am a man of the church, incoherent; I speak of love and I hate myself; I feel sexless and aggressive, but this aggression is well camouflaged. When I was in my parish like Saint-Séverin, I distilled it skilfully, from the pulpit. Greed, sexuality, money, it was all fine. I remember a sermon which was something of a success. I kept the text of it:

"Today I am taking money as a symbol. Money is what disguises our thirst and distracts us from making real sense of our lives. Money is what makes possible the dream of limitless satisfaction, because that is what it promises. And when I say money, I do not just mean money, but also all the good things of life: human success, a profession or married love, a win at the races or a house in the country, reputation or academic distinction. I mean all that, and above all the way in which we experience it; I mean everything that makes possible power, mastery of the future or the domination of others. It is the insurance which paralyses us, the safety rail which holds us in, the idol of happiness which relieves us of the need to live. I take money as the symbol of all that false personal standing which prevents a man from recognizing his poverty. I take it as the symbol of all security which no longer expects anything of the future. I take it as the symbol of everything which permits us to discharge no matter what debt to no matter whom, anything which allows us not to owe anything to anyone. Money makes possible one of man's chief deceits, his attempt to escape from his human condition by trickery."

When I reread this sermon, I cannot see its educative function. I do not believe that by blaming man we allow him to come to terms with his condition. Money can surely be condemned as the essential goal of life. But as for money as a means of making other people happy, as a means of improving the living conditions of those around us, why not? It is as hard to succeed in life as a lay person as it is to succeed as a priest.

If I had to go to work tomorrow to bring up a family, I don't know what I should do. I'm completely incapable. I would find it difficult to move from a diffuse, almost verbal, responsibility to a direct responsibility. In the name of the truth which we have been taught, we have been made tense beings, more capable of judging than of listening or loving. All too often charity is a caricature of love after the style of the Pharisees: "Lord, I am charitable." I cannot bear that expression, "be charitable". I resent it and find it hurtful. The real vocation of the priest is to be someone who communicates: communicates horizontally, but also vertically; that, I believe, is one of the symbolic meanings of the cross. The priest's role is surely not to condemn one person in order to reassure another. We must create places where people can sort themselves out, where they can express themselves freely and criticize their alienations lucidly, communicate with others and rediscover the meaning of their lives. No external structure or bureaucratic arrangement can achieve that. It has to come from within.'

I kept up with this priest for several months. I prescribed tranquillizers for his anxiety and anti-spasmodic drugs for his digestive problems, and I listened to him. He began by venting his aggression on the parish priest who gave him first communion, on his mother, and on his education. One conversation was particularly tricky, that in which he raised the question of the authenticity of his vocation.

'The more I think about it, doctor, the more I feel certain that I did not decide on my vocation freely. What do you think?'

'Be a bit more precise.' (The role of the psychotherapist is not to counsel or direct, but to make the patient reflect and work things out for him or herself.)

'I think that I was put on the rails and followed them without thinking. I gradually built up a personage, an artificial superego, in which I am imprisoned. This "fine figure of a priest" is a cage I want to get out of. For a long time I've play my part to perfection, like a robot. Unfortunately, the mechanism has gone wrong.'

'Why unfortunately?'

'I no longer see the world in the same way, and I no longer want to take refuge in my armour of being the splendid priest.'

'Might you not be able to wear it better?'

'But am I still capable of being a priest?'

'What do you mean?'

'Can a priest live a normal life? I've no desire to have children. I don't feel capable of bringing them up. But I would like to have the right to love a woman without hiding it and without feeling guilty. Father L, one of my old confessors, would say that I want to sell the pig and keep the bacon.'

'Bacon is what makes the pig valuable.'

'It is my vocation to be a man of God in the service of my fellow-men. I think that I will continue to follow my calling as a priest. But why do we not have the right to marry?'

'Is it necessary to be married to love?'

'Obviously not, but we are forbidden sexual intercourse.'

'Have you taken a vow of chastity?'

'Yes, in the sub-diaconate. It wasn't really a vow, it was an agreement. We agreed to be celibate and chaste and we stepped forward a pace to bear witness to our acceptance of this. Basically, the thing I suffer from most is not having had any experience. I have the impression that I could bear chastity more if I had had some love life and sex life before becoming a priest.'

In the course of subsequent conversations we talked a good deal about sexuality. He kept coming back to the problem of his inexperience. More than once he spoke to me of a young single woman who had been working with him for several years. It was clear that he was very much in love with her. One day, he came to our appointment in a very relaxed mood.

'Doctor, I've done it!'

(I did not say anything.)

'I've made love to Anne Marie. . . I have the feeling that I was very clumsy. . . Afterwards, we talked a great deal. She confessed that she had loved me for a long time. I told her that I did not want to get married and that I wanted to remain a priest. She is in complete agreement with me, and is going to continue to work with me. Later, we shall see. For the moment we shall conceal our love. No one in the parish must have any inkling of it. I am certain that one day or another we shall have the right to get married.'

Our conversations became less frequent. In a few weeks I saw a complete change come over this man. He blossomed out, and became full of energy and confidence; now he would only talk about his priestly work.

I have not seen him for a year now. I receive a letter from him every month. He is continuing to build up enthusiastically the house church about which he spoke to me so many times, that place for sharing and exchanging, where the exploiters and the exploited might meet together. A little Christian community has been born. About forty men and women are trying to create occasions for meeting and dialogue. In one of his last letters, he wrote: 'In its role as mediator, this little community is trying to be as far as possible the intermediary between the God of Jesus Christ and people today, the church of yesterday and the church of tomorrow.'

An impotent physics teacher

A man of twenty-six, qualified as a physics teacher, came to consult me about his impotence. Feeling that he was now at last fully grown up, because he was 'a qualified teacher and finished with military service', he had attempted several sexual experiences, with the sole aim of proving that his male organ was capable of something other than masturbation. He was in despair. He had gone with several prostitutes, who were full of good will. They had tried everything, but to no avail. His penis had remained stubbornly flaccid. He had seen what he might achieve locally with one or two girls of more tender years; he liked them to be about eighteen. He had been looked upon favourably up to the point when he had wanted to have intercourse. He was further persuaded that these girls were only in search of marriage: 'A qualified physics teacher is a very valuable commodity on the market.' He had finally taken up with women of about forty, married and on the pill, who therefore were disinterested in every respect. All his efforts were to no avail. He still had erections when he danced, but when he actually 'got down to it', he could not become excited. Flat calm.

As a matter of form, I made all the examinations needed to eliminate any organic origin; the results were perfectly normal. Our first two conversations were devoted to sexual education. His knowledge was limited to what he had learned in natural science about the reproductive mechanisms of the superior mammals. Together we then touched on what for him was a completely unknown world, as we discussed femine psychology and physiology, sexual communication, tenderness and pleasure.

He was sixth in a family of eight children, and had been brought up in excellent surroundings, where Christian principles were the basis of education. His first childhood memory, or at least the one that he could remember most easily, was as follows (he must have been about seven). He was in the garden at home and had a pee. For some time he had been aware that certain kinds of touching were particularly pleasant, and took advantage of the occasion to establish this fact more precisely. Suddenly, his mother appeared and said to him in a severe tone of voice: 'I forbid you to touch that; it's a serious sin, and you must admit to it at confession.' Desire being stronger than this prohibition, he had continued to masturbate, from time to time, in fear and dread of eternal damnation. This problem of masturbation had pursued him throughout his adolescence. On Sunday, the family went to mass *en bloc*. It was unthinkable not to take communion. If, by misfortune, he had masturbated without having had time to confess it, he went to the holy table in the certainty that he had committed a mortal sin. However, he preferred to run this risk rather than put up with the inquisitive glance of his father and the sorrowful attitude of his mother. Not to take communion was officially to acknowledge wickedness.

He went to all his primary classes in a minor seminary. All his education had been dominated by the notion of guilt and sin. Everything was a sin: talking in the dormitory, not going to mass every day (it was not compulsory, but to go to mass and take communion every day was the done thing), not knowing the lessons well, complaining about food, not playing in the playground, going apart with a friend to talk, or playing at jacks during the break. It was vital to run, to play, to be the perfect little pupil who was joining in with all the rest. Not to know the catechism, not to be interested in the subject, and so on, any lack of perfection was punished. The punishment depended on the seriousness of the offence; it might be a reprimand, some prayers in chapel, or extra homework, consisting of copying several passages from the gospels. Particularly serious faults were punished by putting the culprit in the corner, on his knees, hands on head.

A number of basic principles had governed his education.

1. God is everywhere and is watching me every moment of my life. On the day of judgment he will ask me to give account of myself, even of my most hidden actions.

2. We must strive ceaselessly for perfection. That alone permits us to approach God, who is himself perfect.

3. We must forget ourselves, and sacrifice our own desires and needs to the desires and needs of others.

4. We must mistrust our instincts and our evil inclinations. The good Christian must always be alert, because Satan is about, ready to seduce us and to draw us away from God.

The means appropriate for being able to follow such a course of life were as follows: prayer, abstinence, permanent self-sacrifice, daily struggles against evil thoughts, particularly sexual thoughts, and the quest for perfection in every action.

His confessor had often told him, 'God is looking at you and judging you. Think of the sufferings of Jesus Christ crucified. We must learn to die to ourselves.'

'When I think of that period,' he told me, 'I still feel oppressed. That was really a kind of terrorist spirituality.' He went on:

'My parents had very little to do with my education. They had sent me to minor seminary. They had done their duty. My father held an important position in the Banque de France. My mother stayed at home; her eight children kept her fully occupied. We did not really have any communication with my parents. At family meal-times, silence was compulsory. Very often my father listened to the news on the radio, and the least whispering was immediately reprimanded by the stern glance of my mother. We were allowed only to reply to questions which had been put to us: they were concerned with our marks and our places in class. Sometimes my parents had a conversation by themselves. They tended to talk about bits of local gossip. I can never remember having listened to anything but the goings-on of friends and acquaintances.

My father was what I might call a big churchman. He was blameless in every respect. He was kind and courteous to everyone. In actual fact, he was profoundly indifferent. Shut up in his thoughts, living life his own way, he protected himself against all external aggression. He had a well-organized and well-oiled Christian life, made up of regular masses and communions; he paid his clergy dues scrupulously, and gave alms whenever the occasion arose. He was certainly very kind, but too preoccupied with himself and his own existential anxiety to be open to others.

When we were older, and might express some philosophical or religious ideas, he would reply in a peremptory way which brought all conversation to a halt. I can remember having said to him that the church seemed to me to be rather out of date on problems of contraception and abortion. My father flew into a rage and told me in a tone more violent than I had ever heard before, "I forbid you to criticize the church under my roof." He had a well-organized system of thought which made him feel secure. Everything was in its proper place: the hierarchy, the church, the Banque de France. He was a defender of the established order. In fact, he would not allow it to be put in question for a moment. He had too much anxiety of his own to allow himself to be involved in any kind of change. He denied scandal, even if the hierarchy itself were responsible for it. We formed the habit of never expressing in his presence any opinion which might shake his rigid universe. It was useless, and only bothered him. At heart, we were very fond of him. We had nothing against him: he was perfect, but very bad at bringing us up. It was impossible to have a discussion with him and take the opposite point of view: he repressed our aggression completely.

My mother suffered a great deal from my father's attitude. She formed the habit of keeping quiet. Now I can understand how all the ills from which she suffered, migraines, stomach pains, palpitations, were all signs of the suppression of her aggressiveness. Her husband, the great Christian, was very domineering.

Like all good Christian families, we had our oracle: a Dominican father, well-educated and respected. He came to our house once a month for lunch, and we were obliged to submit to his discourses on the social theories of the church. My father always listened respectfully without ever discussing one of his opinions.

During our last conversation you asked me what sexual education I had. I've thought about that. I can sum it up in a few words.

1. Masturbation is forbidden. We were not even allowed to shut the bathroom door when we had a bath. Such an attitude would have been suspect.

2. It is wrong to remove girls' panties. I mention this because my mother's second intervention took place when I was about ten. I had been playing in the garden at home all afternoon with one of my classmates and his two sisters. That evening, my mother asked, "Have you ever taken a girl's panties off? If so, you must say so at confession."

3. Do not spend any time with your friends wearing only underwear. It might give them wicked thoughts. In the junior seminary I was punished for having been around the dormitory in my underwear, though it was only for a few moments.

4. When I was about fourteen, my father gave me the following

advice: mistrust girls, even those who seem to be the most innocent. They are the ones to beware of.

5. The fifth important piece of information was given me by our Sunday oracle: the only permissible form of contraception is the temperature method.

That, in short, was my official and family sex education. As to the rest, I learned what I could. My principal sources of information were the jokes told by my friends and the few pornographic magazines that we passed around. When I look back on my education, I cannot see any place for it there. Squeezed between a religious education made up of prohibitions and a sterile family atmosphere, I did not arrive at any personal reflection on the subject.

Only one thing was left: work. That's what led to my qualification. I feel that my parents are very satisfied and that they think that their education has been crowned with success.

I feel incapable of living in the present; I'm in a perpetual state of anxiety. I brood on the past and I fear the future. I keep finding something for which to blame myself. My imperfections haunt me. I feel incapable of being at the service of others and of submitting to them. I want to live for myself. I often tell myself that I ought to prepare for my eternal life, but in my heart of hearts, I think, "To hell with it."

Even more serious is my difficulty in communicating with other people. Other people are a blockage. I keep asking what they think of me, if they accept me. I had hoped that once qualified as a teacher I would be more at ease. In fact, that has only made it worse. I now keep asking whether people are valuing me for myself or only for my position. When it comes to girls, this kind of thinking creates a complete block. I always have the impression that they want to marry me. I would be a perfect husband; I have all the right qualifications: good family, good education, good training. As you would put it, I regard myself as an object. I feel incapable of expressing my aggression. I feel completely shut up in myself. It makes me refuse the other person, because he always seems to be judging me. I feel dominated by the question, "What will people say?" This "What will people say?" was also the basis of my family education: what óther people think is very important. I never can be myself. I have to preserve my imagé of being a good son, a good pupil, a good Christian, a good qualified physics teacher. I have no self which is unique and all of a piece. I've several selves, and I keep having to bother about these different images. How can I become a person? I often feel a victim. It's this famous object-relationship all over again. I do not succeed in involving myself in my life as a responsible and autonomous being. I would like to have friends, but I do not do what is necessary in order to have them. I always have the impression that people don't like me. My great Christian father is no stranger to this mode of being. I have never seen him personally involved in anything at all. He had no friends, no acquaintances, no social life outside the bank. He lived in isolation, stuffed full of certainties and with his mind fully made up.

The other day you asked me about my emotional relationship with my mother. I've thought about that a good deal. My mother was very affectionate. She cared for us a great deal and made a fuss of us. Unfortunately, she was kept down in very much the same way as we were. After going to a secondary school run by nuns, she stayed at home to learn how to become mistress of the house. I always felt that there were a great many possibilities which she had not realized. For want of anything better, she gave expression to herself in household work, in cooking, and in cakes, at which she was a tremendous success. Her opinion never differed from that of our father. When we asked her for permission to do something a little out of the ordinary, she would always say, "Ask your father."

I read the psychology book you gave me about two weeks ago. I think that I have never got past the Oedipus stage.[1] At the beginning of our conversations I told you that I had attempted intercourse with a forty-year-old woman. When I think back to this episode, I feel that I never really wanted to make love to this woman. I wanted her to kiss me, to caress me, to reassure me. I had a second experience of the same kind. My partner was less patient. Before sending me away, she said, "You mustn't treat me like your mother; you aren't weaned yet." I've also thought about the failures in my experiences with prostitutes. In fact I was obsessed with the risk of VD. It's the only piece of advice my father gave me before I went off on military service: "Don't trust women of easy virtue; they can give you serious diseases, some of which are passed on to children." I know that it's possible to get contraceptives, but I'm incapable of going out to buy them.'

During one of our conversations, I asked my patient about the dominant characteristic of his family circle. Without hesitation, he replied, 'The total absence of communication and real love. Each of us lived in his or her own corner, as best we could.'

As I looked back on the observations of this young man of twenty-six, a number of points struck me. The fact that in a young man, with a brilliant intellect, there could be such a gulf between the intellectual quotient and the psychological quotient. In reading these lines, many people will think: 'That's changed a lot, we've passed that point.' But they will be wrong. I could give them thousands of cases of this kind. Christians have not defined any educational policy. The church continues to use guilt, sin and anxiety as the basis of its education. It still continues to confront the rapid development of social morality with a policy of prohibitions. It reacts slowly and cautiously and always tries to align itself, too late, with the majority opinion.

Another characteristic of the Christian neurosis is the way in which this young man found it impossible to regard himself as an independent person, all of a piece, with his own characteristics. He had learnt a code which he was not to transgress, and his neurotic attitude was particularly marked. He had no confidence in himself and no system of personal values. He was entirely dependent on what other people thought of him. He deliberately refused to give way to them, but the result was the same. He never thought in terms of himself, but only in terms of other people or the figures that they represented. Shut in by his anxiety and his aggression, he went round in a circle, incapable of reflecting on himself, incapable of accepting himself, much less of loving himself. It was impossible for him to pass to adult autonomy. He could not involve himself in his own evolution and responsibility. His ego[2] was governed by external rules which he could not internalize. This rigid superstructure served him as a superego,[3] as an armour in which he found it impossible to move. For him, the essential questions remained: 'Am I guilty under the law? What do people think of me? Am I accepted by others? Do people love me?' This last question is important. It explains why there are so many patients, full of the most various physical symptoms, who haunt doctors' surgeries. A number of these people with so-called 'functional' illnesses are in fact neurotics who are living out an object-relationship in which they always feel unloved. The 'great churchman' has found the solution. He never questions himself and apparently lives at ease in his armour without bothering about finding out what is going on outside. If others break their teeth on it, so much the worse for them! How many of these admirable Christians have made their children into immature, fragile adults, incapable of accepting themselves, irresponsible and aggressive, always looking for an image with which they can identify and which will take them over!

Although this book is not about psychotherapy, I will mention briefly what happened to this budding physics teacher. Like many adolescents brought up in a neurotic milieu, he was caught between desire and defence. He censored his sexual drive in the name of the first things that he had been taught. He confused sexual desire with concupiscence. He thought himself guilty of evil thoughts. On the one hand he had preserved the idealistic image of Mary who had given birth without losing her precious virginity, married to a husband of exemplary chastity. On the other hand, sexual desire was only justified in procreation, which excused carnal desire: 'Increase and multiply.' His psychological tension was aggravated by a complete misunderstanding of women. He thought that the normal sexual act consisted in the penetration of the vagina by the penis, together with a rapid and triumphant ejaculation. One of our first conversations was devoted to female anatomy. With delight he discovered an unknown world: even the names excited him, the mons Veneris, the vulva, the labia majora, the labia minora, the clitoris. He was very interested in the erogenous zones, in the idea of orgasm, in the function of the clitoris. At the same time we discussed sexual communication and pleasure.

His social behaviour developed rapidly. He left home and took a room in town. His relationships with other people were transformed. He got used to listening to them and discovering them without being obsessed by the image he had of himself. He was amazed by the ease with which he made friends.

Rid of his obsession about impotence, he learned not to put sexual intercourse as the priority in all relationships with women. Some weeks after the beginning of our conversations, he made the acquaintance of a young student with whom he began to develop a sexual relationship, with all that that implies of affection, mutual exchange and the discovery of the feminine make-up. They did not make love until several months after their first meeting. For a long time he suffered from premature ejaculation, which was evidence of a certain fear of failure. Relaxation by means of the Schultz method[4] helped him to control his sexuality.

A nun, treated as an object

A nun of about sixty came to consult me about a state of depression, accompanied by writer's cramp. She had found it impossible, for several years, to write normally. After being cured, at my request she wrote her own life-story. I include it here as it was written, word for word.

'I was just twenty when I became a novice. I followed a divine call which I never doubted, and I was resolved to go through with it to the end. Some basic themes kept recurring in the instructions given by the novice mistress: "You are never wrong to obey. You must be faithful in the little things. You must always ask permission." And it was necessary to ask permission for everything: to take a bath twice a month, to wash one's hair, change one's nightdress once a month. It was also necessary to have permission to give or receive the least little thing, even a picture; to write a letter (of course, all the correspondence was censored); to go to bed or get up at a different time from everyone else: recreation, the refectory, the religious office. Permission was even needed to have a conversation with a pupil or a sister. Breaking the rule meant certain traditional penances: kissing the feet of one's sisters; eating meals on one's knees; prostrating oneself full length for all the sisters to walk over; saying a prayer aloud in the refectory with arms outstretched; holding a pencil between one's teeth for a certain time as a punishment for breaking silence; carrying round one's neck the pieces of an article one had been clumsy enough to break. It was the done thing to ask permission to inflict certain mortifications on oneself: self-flagellation with knotted rope, or wearing bracelets made of thorns.

When I think back to this period I am struck by the fact that we were treated as though we were irresponsible, creatures who could not be trusted: the novice-mistress and the Mother Superior could enter our cells without knocking at any time. We had to leave the doors of our cells open to undress: the novice-mistress came to shut them, personally, at nine in the evening. We were not allowed to go out of the garden and we were forbidden to look out of the windows giving on to the street. In the parlour there was always a sister as chaperone. We were not allowed to talk to a priest or a religious outside the confessional. Of course, all that is going back forty-five years, but it is not long since the changes came. This period of the novitiate wasn't the hardest. I followed the path laid down for me with the fixed idea, "The will of the Mother Superior is the will of God." As I wanted beyond all doubt to be faithful to God, or rather to Jesus, I did not raise any questions, and I lived day by day in a kind of unconsciousness bordering on a degree of fatalism. My difficulties began only very much later. I found the emotional solitude very difficult to bear. Being attached to my pupils eased it a bit; I always got on very well with them. I could make them work well and they knew that I understood their little problems. I always taught with liveliness and pleasure. My pupils were attached to me, too. Unfortunately, this in itself was a further source of difficulty. I was not in fact allowed to talk to my pupils outside classroom hours, and I was never to talk to them about anything but their work. That was a great torment, because I had not become a religious in a teaching order simply to transmit the rules of syntax, information about history and geography, or even my love of literature. The attachment which some of my pupils had for me was a cause for suspicion, and I came to dread the tokens of sympathy and popularity which I could not help noting. It is beyond question that more than once the sisters took umbrage at this success and passed on biassed reports to the Superior. When she summoned me, I knew what to expect. So it came about that no sooner had I begun to settle in one house than I was sent on to another. I moved seven times in forty years. Whenever it was possible, other people were given the courses which I liked best and for which I was prepared, i.e. teaching literature in the senior school. So the hours and days of preparation were useless, and I had to adapt myself to younger pupils and teach them things in which I was little interested. Then the time came when private establishments were put under a contract with the state. It was important to draw the most possible out of a valuable teacher, and I was asked to work for a degree. I was very happy to do this, because I have always enjoyed working.

However, once again, they made me go up a dead end: a diploma in Latin when I had never learned Greek. That meant that I could not obtain a full classics degree. Then I took a course for a diploma in French literature, and planned on getting a degree in modern literature, for which the diploma in Latin was no use. Abruptly and unexpectedly, they then suppressed my teaching post. They needed a bursar, and for some reason of which I am unaware, I was nominated. I was forty years old. Overnight, I had to give up all study, all my courses, the teaching which I had always enjoyed. For four years I sat in an office, by myself, confronted with columns of figures, invoices to pay, accounts to draw up. I knew absolutely nothing about it, and because the bursar whom I was replacing had tuberculosis and was in isolation, I could only see her on rare occasions, after all kinds of precautions. Then, one day, the Director was informed that I had begun work for a degree, and I was told: "We need a geography specialist and you must do the work." Despite my delight at being free from my figures and again able to take up teaching, I timidly tried to explain how little interest and skill I had in geography.

I was made to feel that I had overstepped the permitted limit in speaking of my tastes and aptitudes. So I allowed myself to be convinced, and I worked for two other diplomas, which allowed me to have a general degree. Two years later, I learnt that the contract of association required recognized teachers to have a teaching diploma, and in order to be able to continue to teach I had to resume my studies. Two years in England finally allowed me to gain a teaching diploma, at the age of fifty. I was then sent to a school in the north of France, where, as always, I had excellent contacts with the pupils, but I was treated unkindly by the sisters, who found my popularity difficult to take.

That lasted for two years. I was devastated to learn that I had been called to Paris. I hated that city, which was associated with bad memories from my adolescence, and my nervous resistance cracked. That showed itself in a total inability to write, and a pressing need for solitude, which made all communal life impossible. I was in a perpetual state of anxiety, and I had nightmares which I took a morbid pleasure in reconstructing when I woke up.

I had a panic fear of the Mother Superior, a guilt complex, perhaps even a persecution complex, and I was always on the verge of tears. On the other hand, when I was with my pupils I regained my liveliness and my equilibrium. This nervous breakdown was accompanied by a series of very painful liver complaints: the x-rays revealed a stone the size of a hazel-nut blocking my gall bladder. I can remember my relief when I learnt that I was really ill and had to have an operation. Because the nervous depression persisted after the operation, the Mother Superior decided to send me to a psychiatrist.'

I have quoted these comments because they are a good account of the oppression to which numerous religious are subjected. They are regarded as objects to be moved about and used without taking account of their tastes or their aptitudes, supposedly for the greater glory of God.

I followed this sister through psychotherapy. Over a few months, she became aware of all the aggression of which she had felt herself to be the victim. After she had vented all her feelings, she began a long period of reflection which made her certain that she no longer wanted to live in a religious community and that she would no longer accept being pushed around like a child. She obtained permission from Rome to leave the religious life. She had inherited enough money from her family not to have any material worries.

Her dealings with her order are not yet over. Because she is over sixty-five years of age, she asked for a pension for her teaching work. The Superior told her that no contributions had ever been paid for her, and ended her letter, 'In any case, this is not a matter of any importance, because you have enough money to live on.'

Having no reason to let herself be manipulated, our ex-religious, who has now become Madame D, wants compensation. She is even thinking of engaging a lawyer. I might compare these comments with those of a young sister, very intelligent, whom I treated for a stomach ulcer. In the course of our conversations she explained to me how the life which she led at the convent had set off in her a permanent state of anxiety and real crises of anguish. She had to observe the holy rule, ceaselessly examining her conscience, where necessary noting her sins so that she could recall them and confess them to her Superior or in public, all in the name of humility and charity. The Mother Superior alone had the right to take decisions. The older ones were allowed to speak; the young ones had to keep quiet and listen. They had no rights. They were told, 'When you have difficulties, do not think, pray', or, 'Light comes from your Superior and consolation from the tabernacle.'

Sexual information was limited to two great principles. First, never look at men. Whenever a man, a doctor or a workman, came into the house, a bell rang to warn the sisters, who had to hide so as not to see or be seen. It was utterly forbidden to look at a man, close to or from a distance. The second principle governed relations between religious. It followed from the latent horror at possible homosexuality. Religious were forbidden to be together in twos, and the Superior, or a sister delegated by her, had the right to enter the rooms of sisters at any hour of the day or night, without knocking.

The same sister told me that during her apostolic year, the Superior worked out the amount of time that she spent on her knees. During one of our last conversations, she shared with me her worries about the end of the religious life as she had known it.

'With great lucidity, I keep telling myself that things can't go on like this for ever. We are the last survivors of a species which is doomed to extinction. What will take our place? There are no novices; young people are looking for something else. If I were to say that in the community, it would be as though I were mowing everyone down with a machine gun. It needs courage to think about that kind of thing. Doubtless I shall die in an old peoples' home. The old nuns can still hope to die surrounded by their fellow religious, and to be buried in the little community cemeteries, some of which are "high places".'

This young sister decided to learn to be a physiotherapist. She took a course at the Salpêtrière. Now she works in a hospital in the morning and in a dispensary in the afternoon. She is keen on sport, and goes swimming regularly and plays tennis. To make it easier to get around to her various activities she has bought a small car. She lives in an apartment block belonging to the order, in which there are a number of flats. The same key opened all the doors. She changed her lock.

In this way I have helped several sisters to rediscover a place in society by learning a profession or obtaining a qualification. However, this solution works only for the youngest. The older sisters, who have worked as nurses or as teachers without a diploma, have little future. Unless they have some support, how will they live? The sale of land and houses owned by their order is only a short-term solution.

The relaxation of discipline within the major communities presents another problem.[5] It is difficult for older religious, accustomed to a very structured community life, to live together in threes and fours in small apartments. Some of them live alone, rejected by the others, who cannot stand living with them. They could be coped with in a community. Many are full of anxiety and depressed. One of them said to me: 'It's a real breach of contract. I did not become a religious to live by myself. I feel abandoned, and my freedom is choking me.' The decompression has been too brutal.

The hierarchy ought to plan for a regrouping between orders for those religious who want to continue to live in community. As for young postulants, i.e. those who want to enter an order, it is desirable that they should have some training for a job, so that they never find themselves, at a later date, at a dead end.

A married priest

A married priest came to consult me about an anxiety neurosis. When we first met, he put his problem like this:

'I was converted at the age of twenty, and I confused conversion and vocation. With all the ardour of the neophyte, I committed myself to the priesthood. At the age of forty I left the priesthood and married. I confused wanting to make love and wanting to get married. Now I feel completely lost. I have children, a job which does not interest me in the least, and I feel incapable of adapting to normal life. I feel incapable of imposing myself. I have no professional qualification. I've found work as a laboratory assistant. I'm obsessed with material problems: I can't make ends meet.

From my training in seminary and as a priest I've kept a desire to be a perfectionist, which drives me on. I can't get rid of it. My twenty years as a priest have refined my sensibility and have developed in me a certain capacity for understanding people, two qualities which a technological society does not really need. I would like to have worked as a receptionist, but that is extremely difficult. I have no papers, no diploma, and I have to be content with a manual job, for which I have no aptitude.

I now feel guilty at not having been able to cope with my priesthood or my celibacy. I feel guilty at having married, guilty at not being able to earn my living properly. I always have the feeling that other people are looking at me with a scornful air, that they're judging me.'

'Do you really believe what you've just told me?'

'Yes and no. My intellect tells me that it's my sense of guilt which makes me feel like this, but that doesn't prevent me from feeling overwhelmed by the opinion of others. It's as though I have a record going round and round in my head: "They know that you've been a priest, that you've not been able to keep your promises. They're scornful of you." I know that that's just not true of the majority of people around me. When I got married, all my friends came to my help.'

'And your bishop?'

'He was very paternal. He asked me to reflect and pray. I went into retreat. In fact I couldn't bear the emotional solitude. I was in a suburban parish, with a vicar of about sixty, very holy, but very silent. We never talked together. I was involved in teaching the catechism and in Catholic Action. I had no way of recharging my batteries.'

'How did you get to know your wife?'

'I was teaching her the catechism.'

'You fell head over heels in love?'

'That's hard to say. I think that in fact I discovered women. I had never had such a close psychological relationship with a woman. When I was at school I always worked very hard. I was a good, industrious pupil. My father and mother were lay teachers. For them, school results were what counted. We never had any close personal relationship. My parents were too involved in their work.

For them, my good marks were the sign of a good education. When I was eighteen, I went as monitor to a colony holiday. The priest in charge of this was an extraordinary person. For the first time, I met an enthusiastic grown-up who, to use your language, was the first father image with whom I could identify.'

'Did he direct you towards the priesthood?'

'Not at all. He didn't give me any advice; but I wanted to be like him. For me, the gospel of Christ was a discovery to be passed on. I was training to be a teacher. Although I didn't really have the vocation, I was in the first year of training college. The son of teachers, I wanted to become a teacher: in fact, I had no information which would allow me to choose any other work. I was set on that particular path.'

'How old were you when you were converted?'

'Nineteen.'

'Did you go to a seminary straight away?'

'When I was twenty. I worked for a year as a teacher in order to think about it.'

'Did this year help you to decide?'

'Above all, I was bored to tears. I was teaching seven-year-olds. I really think that teaching wasn't my vocation. I should have worked in an adult world as a worker or employee. Taking a post as a teacher was the easy way out.'

'How did your parents take the decision to enter a seminary?'

'Not very well. They saw their son as a university lecturer.'

'How did they react?'

'They were disappointed. They tried to talk to me, but it was too late to start a dialogue.'

'Did you find your seminary training interesting?'

'In retrospect, no. I was not trained for the work of a priest in a changing world. The education might have been enough twenty years earlier.'

'Why?'

'I wasn't trained to live in this changing society. We had two courses on Marxism and one on psychoanalysis, and a number of courses on modern developments in religion and the idea of God: what one might call secularization.'

'Secularization?'

'There is a gulf between traditional religious life and modern ways of living and thinking.'

'But shouldn't these courses have been interesting?'

'We only touched on the problem. I dreamed of being a worker priest, but the prohibition from Rome came before I could enter the Mission de France.'

'Do you regret that?'

'Yes and no. I see so many friends who have emerged from their experience as worker priests disgusted and sometimes shattered.'

'Why?'

'It's always the same reason: lack of preparation. Worker priests should have had intensive training in politics, sociology and even psycho-analysis. Classical theological training is far from being enough. They came up against people stronger than they were.'

'And then?'

'Some left, others were dismissed. When the team was united, it was possible, but not for those in isolation. It's difficult not to let oneself be carried away.'

'Carried away by what?'

'Some became Marxists, and no longer think of anything but politics and the class struggle. They've lost their sense of vocation. I have always seen the priest as a communicator, a link between people. Priests aren't needed to run trade unions.'

'Why not?'

'It's not their job. Workers don't need them to get organized. Political parties can organize themselves better than any priest.'

'What does the worker expect of the priest?'

'Something that we can't provide. A culture, and a spiritual open-mindedness which makes sense of their lives.'

'What do you feel to be the sense of your life?'

'That's a difficult question. I would like to say love, but that hides a multitude of things: education, culture. It's easier to be a politician than to teach intelligently. During my time in the seminary I suffered a good deal from a certain negation of culture: it was thought to be middle-class. To be near to the workers it was necessary to be like them. I think that is wrong: workers want to be brought something. They love to learn. People really advance through culture. If priests haven't learnt that, they're nothing but feeble understudies.'

'Understudies of whom?'

'People whose job it is to engage in politics and continue the class struggle.'

'In your view, what is the place of the priest in modern society?'

'To be a man of love and an educator in the widest sense of the term.'

'Is training nowadays developing in this direction?'

'Not at all. The hierarchy is too preoccupied with the internal reforms of the church, and at the same time it is obsessed with the idea of not losing the working-class clientèle.'

'Clientèle?'

'Yes, I used that word deliberately. The church has become a demagogue. On the one hand, it doesn't really reflect on the big problems like sexual education, the pill, abortion, woman's place in society, the development of working-class culture, the use of leisure. Youth movements are disappearing one after the other. Of course they were out-of-date, but I think that young people need others to educate them and enthuse them. I would like to have been a school chaplain or a college chaplain. Impossible. The traditional parish structure had to be kept up, and we didn't have enough manpower. The rigidity of its structures had to be respected. If a school or college chaplaincy had developed alongside our parish, a good part of the clientèle would have left. The young people take their parents with them. They go to mass at the school, they take part in the meetings and the activities at the chaplaincy.'

'Isn't that a good development?'

'Not for the parish priest.'

'Why not?'

'He sees his congregation disappear. The chaplaincy is there among young people, at the heart of things. The parish priest, in his church, waits for people to come. This structure has perished.'

'Just fine ceremonies in a beautiful monument?'

'Not even that. The liturgical reforms have put the cart before the horse. Most Sunday masses are lamentable. In the chaplaincies, the young people, living together, can produce something beautiful. In the churches, Bach has been replaced with songs full of squawks. . .'

'Are you an integralist?'

'Not at all, but I think that people have changed the form before the substance. The hierarchy did not shift for fifty years, and then it took the plunge without sufficient thought. Papal infallibility is not enough to arrange things.'

'Are you against papal infallibility?'

'A difficult question. I wish the Pope would use his authority to change the training of priests and their status in society. Why does he not call for in-depth political, social and sexual education in the seminaries? Why doesn't he declare that the priest has a right to a sexual life? To come back to my problem: when I came to know Françoise, I discovered the joy and the equilibrium which a sexual relationship gave me. I mean a sexual relationship and not sex. I was unprepared. The reaction of the parishioners didn't help. They began to whisper in corners. Our relationship became suspect: the fact that we often talked together and that we were alone together in my study was interpreted in the worst possible way. My vicar received anonymous letters. It made me furious. Let me make it quite clear: we didn't have sexual intercourse until we were married. The attitude of the Christian community determined my choice. There again I felt oppressed.'

'Oppressed by what?'

'By Christians. The priest is an asexual being. That reassures all these good middle-class men and women who are ashamed of their sex, while thinking about it too much. One of the worst faults of the church is having introduced a guilt-complex about sex. Little by little, Françoise and I came to feel guilty and isolated. There were only two possible solutions: break it off, or get married. At the start, I told you that I confused wanting to make love and wanting to get married. That was an aggressive way of presenting things. For two whole years, we never wanted a sexual relationship. The hypocritical attitude of the majority of the parish bolstered up our relationship, and, yes, we wanted to make love. It's difficult to spend two years on a desert island.'

'A desert island?'

'Many adults treated us as though we had the plague. There were enough innuendos. And yes, ! wanted to make love to Françoise. I decided to marry her.'

'Did the hierarchy react?'

'Not really. I found a great deal of paternalism, but I came up against a block. A retreat was no use. I would have liked to remain as a priest and live with Françoise, but I didn't really want to start a family and have children. I retained my vocation to be at everyone's disposal, to the availability of the priest. I would like to have continued to work with young people. As a family man, working as a laboratory assistant, that's difficult.'

'Do you regret your marriage?'

'Not really. I regret my priestly profession. My only obsession now is that of making both ends meet. Françoise will have to find a job. I wish that could have been avoided when the children are so small. Next year I've asked for a post as a teacher, and I hope to become qualified to teach literature. It's going to be hard, but I must find some way out.'

'Do you feel depressed?'

'More than ever, and in addition, I begrudge having given way to the pressure of an infantile Christian community.'

'Do you still practise?'

'Yes, but not in the traditional structures. I and other married priests have formed a small community. We meet regularly and share in the eucharist.'

'If priests were allowed to marry one day, what would you do?'

'As things are, I would go back to my work as a priest. In ten years' time, I don't know. For the moment, I would like to be able to accept life as it is. Without anxiety and without guilt. I must be reconciled to myself.'

Psychotherapy allowed this priest to be reconciled with himself. He came to realize that the real problem was neither his marriage nor his material difficulties: he had been the victim of a complete lack of education. The first adult with whom he had communicated, and on whom he had wanted to model himself, had been a priest. This encounter had been decisive. He identified with the priest, but did not really have a vocation. He also suffered a great deal from his lack of preparation for modern life. In the seminary, he had again come up against the rigid structures of his family circle: sin had taken the place of bad marks.

He rejected developments in the church which he described as 'demagoguery for the workers'. He also became aware of his aggression towards the clerical hierarchy and his rejection of prohibitions against sex and the association of guilt feelings with it. In the end, he discovered that working as a teacher allowed him to have just as large a role in education as the priest.

He took a job as a teacher and obtained a diploma in literature. He became involved with a group of young people looking for a new spirituality and entered a charismatic group.

He has really come out of his depression, and resolved his inner conflicts by discovering the real causes of his aggression and his anxiety. He has rediscovered the keys to his own life story.

A practising Catholic doctor

Even doctors can be psychologically ill. Like priests, their training is often inadequate for coping with the modern world. They are trained to treat symptoms, but not sickness, the integral element of the life-story of those who are ill. A number of my colleagues have come to discuss these problems: harrassed, disgusted with their profession which is limited to treating symptoms bit by bit, they feel that their work is superficial, ending up only in the progressive organization of sickness, far less dealing with it in psychiatric terms.

A doctor of about fifty came to see me for a phobic neurosis. His first troubles had presented themselves while he was driving round on visits in his car: dizziness, anxiety, oppression had forced him to stop for more than an hour. These phobias grew progressively worse: as he told me at our first meeting, he could not bear crowds and noise, and he became panic-stricken in traffic jams, in the underground, and even at Sunday mass. He could foresee the time when he would no longer be able to go out. His story was a simple one. Brought up in a classic Christian family, very well structured, he had learned the morality of submission at a very early age. He had been brought up in a Catholic school, and then by the Jesuits. In his view, if one were being educated by the Jesuits, there were only three possible solutions: to be ferociously anti-clerical, to become a Jesuit, or to be ground down. Unfortunately, though without meaning to do so, he had chosen the third course. He had become a good Christian, a good family man and a traditional, utterly legalistic doctor. He honestly practised the Christian ethic of black and white, good and evil, and projected this image as far as he could on his clientèle. So he was confronted with impossible situations.

Our conversations were essentially concerned with the nature of these situations. The most difficult problem was that of abortion. In order to obey the moral law, he had always abandoned (and I use the word advisedly) all the young women or wives who wanted an abortion for social or psychological reasons. One of them, mother of a family, had died of acute septicemia and nephritis following an abortion by a nurse which was carried out in particularly dramatic circumstances. This death particularly troubled him, because he felt responsible for it. In fact he had only obeyed his legalistic Christian conscience, and he had not committed any sin!

For him, contraception was a no less agonizing problem: he had continued to advise the rhythm method or coitus interruptus, though he knew their limitations and their imperfections. He knew that the practice of coitus interruptus made a certain number of men impotent. 'Unfortunately I did not have any other solutions to offer them.' This method is particularly difficult to practise. The man has to control his erection, not release the least drop of spermatic fluid, and withdraw at the last moment. Where is the joy or the release in sexual intercourse and communication with that kind of method?

Another problem distressed him: whether or not he should tell the patient the truth. On the one hand the Christian law forbade him to lie; on the other hand, the patient had the right to the whole truth. In the course of our conversation I told him the story of a monk suffering from cancer of the pancreas. He arrived at the hospital as yellow as a quince. Surgical examination revealed a tumour in the pancreas blocking the hepatic ducts. The surgeon was content with by-passing the tumour: the result of the operation was spectacular. In four days the patient had lost his yellow tinge, and he regained his normal weight in a month. Six months later, he returned with his Superior for a consultation: he was flourishing. The Superior took me on one side and said, 'Have you told him the truth?' 'No, it's pointless. All is going well.' 'You must tell him the truth, he's a good man.' 'Father Superior, you must decide. I personally refuse.' 'Very well, I shall tell him myself.' Two weeks later, we heard that the monk had died.

Can a doctor afflicted with the Christian neurosis really do his job? The doctor must be at the service of his patients, and must not project his own anxieties and his own taboos on them. He is responsible for their lives and their mental balance. A Christian doctor who allows an abortion to be carried out in any conditions whatsoever shares in the responsibility for the death of his patient. A doctor who does not explain clearly all the methods of contraception, their advantages and their inconveniences, is not doing his job. Doctors must break away from a neurotic education and learn to judge and appreciate for themselves the necessity of this or that attitude or decision. They are on their own, faced with their patients, and the only law which they have to obey is that of their patients' interests.

The doctor whom I have just mentioned ended up by being unable to go to mass. He was overcome with dizziness and nausea which compelled him to leave. Fortunate symptoms which obliged him to take stock and discover that his Christian neurosis was incompatible with carrying on his profession! In the course of our conversations, he put forward a particularly interesting idea. 'Sometimes I have the impression that my patients come to me to ask for absolution.' He felt that the symptoms for which his patients came to consult him concealed an anxiety which he had to calm: a conscientious examination, detailed questioning always ended up with the same conclusion: 'There's nothing wrong with you. I will give you some pills and then all will be well.'

'I know,' he said, 'that all these people are asking me for something else: their symptoms are a cry for help to which I am unable to respond. I really do have the impression of giving them absolution; my prescription takes the place of the three Hail Marys or three Our Fathers which a parish priest would give them. I have the impression of being just like the priests: conscientious and incompetent. Very often they, too, give absolution, knowing that the real problem isn't there.

Last Easter I went to confession: the priest was even quicker than the general practitioner. Each confession lasted two or three minutes, all in all. He got through about twenty patients, sorry, twenty sinners, an hour. With me he broke all records: I hardly had time to get down on my knees, and he gave me the absolution before I had time to speak. He must have been exhausted and perhaps disgusted. This confession reminded me of some surgeries in the winter when one got through twenty patients with influenza in an hour. No need to listen to them; all the patients had the same thing. I often recall this priest, who said to me, "They tell me all the same rubbish." '

I couldn't help bursting out laughing, because this story reminded me of a patient who had come away from his doctor holding up his trousers: he hadn't had time to do up his braces.

The more I reflect, the more I think that doctors and priests have the same lack of psychological training. The former cope with problems by prescriptions, the latter by absolutions. In both cases the aim is the same: reassurance. But can doctors and priests who do this kind of work, whether they like it or not, be content with themselves? What solution can we offer them if they cannot cope with their work? General practitioners always have the possibility of specialist work which allows them to continue some kind of objective medicine without guilt and without anxiety. Priests do not have the same solution. They do not have any training which allows them to do a job which matches their cultural level. I know priests who have become craftsmen, taxi drivers, building workers. I also knew one who committed suicide.

How did I deal with this practising Catholic doctor? It was very easy. I advised him to supplement his formal medical training with a course in psychology: a Balint group and some group dynamics. In group dynamics, under the direction of a psycho-analyst, he learned how to question himself by studying his own reactions and the real motivation behind his behaviour. In this way he discovered that his communication with others began from communication with himself, and that self-analysis called for consideration of others.

The Balint group enables him to study along with his colleagues the development and treatment of a certain number of patients whose observations are considered together. The psychoanalyst present at the sessions helps general practitioners to a better understanding of the reasons which make them take one decision or another when confronted with a difficult patient.

He learned, too, that often the doctor-patient relationship is not an assymetrical one (teacher-taught or master-pupil), but that it is a real means of communication.

I saw him again some months later, and found him very relaxed. He told me that his medical practice had completely changed.

'Often the patient does the talking and I keep quiet. I try to understand him and put myself in his place. I've become aware that numerous symptoms are due to unexpressed psychological problems. My job has become more difficult, but I'm not complaining. I no longer feel as if I'm doing just anything.'

2

Confession and the Good Conscience

A missionary of about forty came to consult me for recurring eczema of the anus, which forced him to keep scratching himself, regardless of time or place. A psychoanalyst would immediately have suspected the repression of certain homosexual fantasies; however, a rapid clinical examination allowed me to diagnose haemorrhoids, and treatment by a proctologist put an end to the eczema. I remained on friendly relations with this priest, and he came back to see me several times for the pleasure of a discussion. On our first meeting, when he learned that I was writing a book to be called *The Christian Neurosis*, he said to me:

'The term "Christian neurosis" interests me. I followed the classical pattern: a Christian family and minor seminary. I have the impression of being made up of a series of different layers: the lowest layer consisting of anxiety and guilt, that is, the family layer. As a child, I was obsessed by the sin which I had to confess at family prayers in the evening, preceded by what I would call "a spoken examination of one's conscience". The second layer is a layer of repression: at minor seminary I was obsessed by sexual sin. I often remember having been punished because I was reading a small illustrated magazine at the bottom of the garden, hidden behind a tree. The watcher who discovered me slapped me a couple of times, and told me, "You dirty swine, you've been hiding to masturbate." In the evening I had to spend the whole of dinner on my knees with my hands behind my head. The third layer is a layer of oppression: in the novitiate we were put under very strict discipline, and communication was virtually impossible. Silence was one of the golden rules of our training (I hardly dare call it education). Our life was governed by the blessed clock. Now things have changed, and our communities are more lively, but between priests of my generation there is embarrassment and a difficulty in communication which I believe to be definitive.'

'If I understand you properly, your ego, as Freud would put it, is made up of a mixture of anxiety, guilt, repression and oppression. And your superego?'

'My superego . . . is being built up gradually. My work as a missionary helps me, but I think that I shall always have anxiety-feelings and guilt-feelings about everything, to no purpose. What is impressed on one's conscience at a very early stage is there for ever. The first mark seems to me to be indelible. However, I am able to help and reassure the Christians for whom I am responsible. I try to teach them love and to minimize as far as possible all the little daily happenings which make up by far the greatest majority of their sins.'

'Oughtn't you to be able to free yourself from your anxiety and your guilt feelings by confession?'

'Yes, that has often relieved me a good deal.'

'Relieved you? Like taking an aspirin for toothache?'

'If you like to put it that way. The act of confessing removes the weight of a grief which is sometimes intolerable.'

'But the cause?'

'That's the problem. Confession has its limitations at the causal level: it does not cure the dental decay. Confession is enough for a small toothache, minor neuralgia which is not caused by any lesion. I find your comparison interesting: it is aspirin for guilt, but when there's something more important, it does not deal with it in depth. It's enough to be pardoned if one is truly contrite, but it is not enough to repent if one is to be capable of changing profoundly, to begin to understand the reason for one's attitudes.'

'The well-oiled stereotypes of neurosis!'

'What do you mean?'

'I mean that an education based on sin produces in those who undergo it stereotyped attitudes which always bring them back to the same problems. The kind of confession which is practised does the most to encourage the Christian neurosis, because it is superficial and treats people as infants. That is, because it is enough to confess to a representative of the Father to be pardoned. As a matter of form, he gives you several automatic prayers to recite. But the pardon of the priest, the representative of God, is not enough to bring freedom from all problems. Confession is superficial because it does not help those who submit to it any further forward.

For example, take the problem of masturbation which you mentioned to me just now. It's wrong even to consider masturbation systematically as a sin: in the majority of cases, it is an action corresponding to a normal state of evolution in an adolescent, or to a need to compensate for emotional frustration or sexual problems. Sometimes it is a very simple physiological need among those who are committed to celibacy or chastity. In exceptional cases there may be a form of compulsive or obsessive masturbation which is part of a pathological state; in that case it calls for a specialist doctor and not a priest (I knew a youth who masturbated ten times a day). In all these instances I see no role for a priest, far less for confession. A well-conducted psychological interview might lead the person involved to understand the reason for his attitude and to find the means of remedying it.

Suppose we take some other examples. A small boy steals jam or sweets: confession is no use. It's much more interesting to know why the child steals. Contrary to the ideas impressed on us by classical Christian education, the child is not marked by sin from his or her birth. It's far too easy to say, "Man is born a sinner, God forgives him, and thanks to baptism, confession, etc., he can become a child of God again and remain so." In fact, confession is simply the indispensable corollary of education based on prohibition and guilt. An open education, based on love and responsibility, would produce very different results.'

Among my patients I have many problem couples, and many of the couples, indeed by far the greatest majority of them, are Christians. Why? Don't the others have any problems?

Certainly, but they are not the same. Christian couples find it more difficult than others to divorce, and in itself that is a good thing. Divorce is always a trauma for the children. They come to me to see what has happened and to re-establish real communication: very often, their basic problem is sexual. They are castrated[6] at the level of pleasure and joy. Whenever I give a lecture on sexual education, I never confine myself to the study of the reproductive function among superior vertebrates. I always insist on the fact that it is important to give children the idea of sexual communication and the joy and pleasure associated with it at a very early age.

I am struck by the sexual guilt of the Christian couples who come to consult me. Many of them are still at the stage of 'inner conflict', without a third person. Sometimes the husband is impotent, either completely, or with premature ejaculation. Sometimes – and this happens most often – the wife is apparently frigid. One of my patients told me that she was very worried because she could not do her marital duty. This expression 'marital duty' is one of the many inspirations of the church. The only solution to which this woman had been able to have recourse, up to our first interview, had been to accuse herself at confession. The response was always the same: 'You must do your conjugal duty.' This injunction had been accompanied by one of those stereotype discourses that you often hear in traditional confessions: 'Think of the sufferings of Christ on the cross, think of the Virgin Mary, and so on. God understands and knows our sufferings; his love is immense and he pardons everything. Pray. You must recite three Our Fathers and two Hail Marys.'

Unfortunately, prayer has never cured frigidity. Psychological consultation allowed the patient to discover the reason for her behaviour: a profound disgust of sexuality. As she said to me one day, 'It's dirty; sperm disgusts me. I cannot bear my husband caressing my clitoris. I have the impression of committing a sin against purity.'

'Basically, you refuse to play.'

'Yes.'

'Why?'

'I've always thought that the sexual act was necessary for the man, and that the woman had to submit without getting any pleasure from it.'

'Who taught you such ideas?'

'It's a conclusion that I drew from my education. The sisters always told us to mistrust men, because all they were after was to take advantage of women. I've kept the idea that the sexual act should be only for procreation. No one ever told me that pleasure and joy should be associated with it.'

'Do you feel pleasure when your husband caresses you?'

'None at all. I just long for it to be over and for him to get his relief.'

'Is that the only reason why you accept sexual intercourse?'

'Yes, my mother always told me that I must never refuse my husband.'

'Why?'

'In case he went elsewhere. . .'

I can't see how confession can sort out that kind of problem. . .

Let me quote another case. A man came to consult me about

impotence. His erection was normal, but as soon as he tried to penetrate the vagina, his penis suddenly went limp. He was very guilty about not being able to satisfy his wife.

The couple had two children, and the wife, whom I met several days later, explained that she did not know how she could have become pregnant. From time to time her husband succeeded in ejaculating without really penetrating. After a long journey, some particularly vigorous spermatazoa had reached their destination.

The history of this man of thirty was as follows: prolonged masturbation without any relationships, even sentimental, with women, before he came to know his wife. He had married at twenty-five: he was a scout leader, and had met his wife when she was in charge of the cubs in the same parish. At first he had thought of being a priest, and had spent a year at major seminary. In addition to the sexual inhibitions which he had kept from his education, he felt guilty at not having continued towards the priesthood. In fact he was castrating himself to punish himself. He did not have the right to play. There again, we rediscover the notion of the illegality of pleasure. Of course, the church now has much less rigid positions. But that is not enough to enable generations deformed by its education to rediscover normal behaviour overnight.

Confession is the indispensable complement of Christian education. No growth is possible through sin and guilt. If a prohibition is transgressed, the culprits must rapidly put themselves right with God. Transgression is as indispensable for growth as renunciation. However, transgression and renunciation are valuable only if the subject who experiences them is capable of understanding why he or she is transgressing or renouncing. If they undergo all that they experience without understanding, they go round in circles and remain feeble beings, victims of an alternation of sins and confessions which allow them to survive. Others construct an artificial superego, rigid and moralizing, and become integralists or anti-integralists, or perhaps Jehovah's Witnesses or paratroopers, which allows them to externalize their anxiety and their aggression. Others, finally, become phobic. They are victims of their irrational, obsessive, anxious fears; they are afraid of wide open spaces, afraid of being shut up, afraid of blushing, and so on. Their anxiety and their repressed aggressiveness turn them in on themselves and, as Freud says, 'the lines of force in their personalities deteriorate'. Always tense, they wait more or less consciously for the just punishment of their wickedness. They cannot bear the looks of others, who ceaselessly criticize and judge them. They have dizzy spells in the street (dizzy spells isn't quite right; they have the impression of emptiness in their head and a fear of falling). They are oppressed, they have palpitations or nausea. They feel under constant attack. Some of them justify this impression by the fact that they are misunderstood and are not accepted or loved by anyone. It is a pity that confession does not cure these phobic symptoms, which are the externalization of a profound anxiety.

As 'the practising Catholic doctor' said, confession, as it is practised now, is similar to certain procedures which the general practitioner carries out under pressure. The person involved, treated as an object, with his prescription or his absolution, finds himself purged of every symptom, or of his sin, without having had time really to explain himself. The same as before, he goes off towards another sin, another symptom and another confession, without having progressed a millimetre.

'But what do you make of sacraments?', someone may ask.

A priest once said to me: 'There is no very great difference between one's approach to a doctor and one's approach to a confessor. Both consist in giving a clear account of one's ailment with a desire to be cured of it. By contrast, the responses are essentially different. The doctor responds by human means to an ailment for which there is a human treatment. The sacrament responds by supernatural means to an evil from which it is impossible to be liberated without the intervention of Christ.'

Unfortunately for many Christians, the sacrament of penitence is a simple rite. They do not confess in order to understand the reasons for their behaviour, and to change it. They come to put themselves right with the law. To be persuaded of this, one only has to look at the crowd which throngs the churches on the eves of major festivals. The priests, completely run off their feet, distribute absolution by rotation.

A theologian whom I asked about the problem of confession told me: 'The psychological cure frees a patient from anxiety and guilt and enables him to rediscover contentment and equilibrium. The sacrament of penance makes a man understand all his wretchedness. He knows that he is a sinner and that he will always remain one.'

As a doctor, I cannot see myself saying to my patients, 'You are sick and you will always remain so. Come and see me, and I will give you a prescription to relieve the symptoms.' It is true that whereas it is enough to confess one's sins to be pardoned, it is not enough to list one's symptoms to be cured. Numerous Christians use the priest in the same way as patients use the doctor: to obtain relief by being involved as little as possible. The real cure is growing more mature: it requires man-as-object, in the security of his rites or his drugs, to leave his infantile dependance and become man-as-subject, capable of understanding why he is anxious, why he is a sinner, why he is sick.

Among Christians, the way in which confession has classically been practised has developed what one might call 'a good conscience'.

'I am all right with God, with the law; I can continue to live in peace without questioning myself.' In ancient Christianity, public penance (there was no other kind) was edifying. Later, from the sixth to the twelfth century, it was strictly costed out. Fasting, living on bread and water for months or years, long pilgrimages barefoot, imprisonment, flogging, heavy fines . . . these were all penalties which had to be undergone before receiving absolution. One may indeed grant that these techniques of absolution cured people of feeling like indulging in a 'good sin'. However, rather than make such penances the order of the day, it would be easier to change the training of priests. Like all illnesses, sin can be a factor in growth. When a child steals, lies or rebels, he has profound reasons for stealing, lying or rebelling. When a grown-up transgresses the principles which he has theoretically accepted as the foundation for his behaviour, it is because he has profound reasons for doing so. I wish that priests had enough psychological training to be able to understand what penitents wanted to tell them. For that, it is indispensable to abandon the priest-sinner relationship, which makes people infantile, just as it is necessary to abandon the similar doctor-patient relationship, which allows the perpetration of magical, expeditious, superficial . . . and noxious actions.

A good conscience, easily acquired, is one of the consequences of absolution quickly given. This good conscience is a remarkable mode of defence. It makes possible the discovery of a balance when one has received an education which prevents one from living with oneself. It is difficult for people to love when they do not love themselves; it is difficult to serve simultaneously a religion of love and a consumer society oriented on money. Finally, it is difficult to defend truth and justice in the framework of the structured religious institution, hierarchical and integrated, which is no more than a replica of capitalist society. The good conscience is the way out for the legalist Christian, who thus finds a compromise between the theoretically unconditional law of love and the compromising situations in which he is obliged to live.

I recall a meeting which brought together final-year pupils and their parents: a father, managing director of a business firm, was explaining with the utmost seriousness that the difference between Christians and others was that they had a moral sense: 'We Christians know what we are doing; we are willing to pass under the Caudine forks of capitalism, but we are aware of the fact.' A pupil, somewhat stunned by this declaration, said, 'I thought that the difference between Christians and others was that they believed in the risen Christ.' An embarrassed silence fell on those present. Courageously, the chaplain spoke: 'The difference between Christians and others is that they know that they are children of God and that they too are promised the resurrection.'

Another pupil got up: 'Do you really think, Father, that Christians are the only ones to have a moral sense?'

'No, I think that many non-Christians are honest and conscientious.'

'Will they be raised again?'

'God alone will judge that.'

That's a good reply. When one does not know what to say next, one simply replies, 'God alone will judge that.' It is a pity that doctors haven't developed the habit of replying to anxious patients who ask whether they will get better, 'God only knows.'

Many Christians, even very intelligent ones, have a particular view of the world: a world totally ordained and willed by God. In this connection I remember a discussion which I had with a very well-qualified engineer. We touched on the problem of war.

'How would you explain the war in Biafra, in connection with God and the economy of creation?'

'God willed this war.'

'That's obvious, why didn't I think of it? Everything is in place: war, peace, illness, the death of a child, a road accident, and so on. Why worry? God does all things well. He sends us a little war from time to time to remind us that he exists.'

'All these tests are sent us by God to counterbalance the sin of the world.'

'Do we all share in this sin?'

'Yes, and to avoid being punished, we must keep right with God.'

'What do you do to keep right with him?'

'I make sure that I never remain in a state of sin. The sacrament of penance is a means given us to reconcile ourselves with God.'

'And how are you reconciled with yourself? How can you bear to hold such an important position in a business which lives by exploiting under-developed peoples?'

'It is hard for me to justify a whole business. I am not the owner; I am only one of the directors. I do my duty conscientiously in the place where God has put me.'

'I did not think of that solution. You are perfectly programmed. God made you enter the polytechnic, he gave you the post of director in a business which exploits the under-developed. You do your duty well without asking questions. I understand: it's your only way of having a good conscience.'

A woman came to consult me for persistent insomnia.

'How long has it lasted?'

'About two months.'

'Are you in distress?'

'Yes.'

'What happened?'

'It's hard to tell you.'

After a few moments of silence, the young woman said to me in a barely audible voice:

'I went to bed with a priest.'

'Yes . . . and you feel guilty?'

'No.'

'Then why are you in distress?'

'Because I went to bed with him.'

'Ah!'

'Before that, he was pure, and now he's not.'

'Have you broken with him?'

'We break about every two weeks.'

'Why?'

'Because he comes back when he can't bear it any longer.'

'And then you go to bed again?'

'Yes.'

'And the next day, he wants to break with you?'

'Yes.'

'Don't you think that you're also responsible for this situation?'

'Yes, but I love him.'

'What about him?'

'I don't know. He tells me that he loves me when he wants to go to bed with me.'

'And afterwards?'

'Afterwards, he calls me a whore. He has even told me that I'm harming his priestly vocation. He's a priest and he wants to remain one.'

'In fact, he holds you entirely responsible?'

'Yes.'

'What does he say to you?'

'That he forgives me, that he understands my weakness, but that I must think of my husband, that I must remain faithful. . . He has also told me, "It is in forgetting that one discovers and it is in giving that one receives." '

'If I understand you rightly, he is asking you to give yourself to him when he needs to make love and then to forget that you have been to bed with him and that you love him.'

'Exactly. When he comes back to see me, because he has a very urgent sexual desire, he tells me: "You can't refuse me that. I know that I'm a poor sinner, but I know that you understand me, and I'm sure that I can count on your discretion." The next day, the same scene begins all over again: he puts me out of his study, and calls me all sorts of names.'

'And do you continue to accept such a situation? Don't you find that your priest-lover lets himself off rather too lightly by blaming you?'

'Perhaps, but I love him. I've come to see you because I've stopped sleeping. All night I brood and think about him. Yesterday, he told me that he liked my husband very much and could not understand why I deceived him. I don't know where I am any more.'

'Would I be right in thinking that he made love to you the day before yesterday?'

'No, three days ago.'

I find this priest's defence system remarkable. He is not the only one to use it: a very distinguished superior told me that from time to time he went to bed with the mother of a pupil because it was the only way in which she could bear her husband. One service deserves another. A good conscience is an excellent way of avoiding guilt. I had a good deal of difficulty in treating this 'young insomniac who went to bed with a priest'. The more serious of the two invalids wasn't in my study.

In the course of her conversations she became aware of her own responsibility. She had been attracted by this priest, not only because he was handsome (the idol of the parish), but also and above all because he was a priest: he represented untouchable man, difficult to seduce, the father in whom one could trust, the director of consciences and . . . the Christ.

She also reflected on her relations with her husband. She had a good deal of regard and affection for him, but physically he did not attract her. She said he was a good husband and a good father, but a bad lover, although, in contrast to the priest, he did not regard her as an object of pleasure. He paid her a good deal of attention.

She gradually came closer to him and found in him a number of qualities of which she had not been aware (even that of making love well). In a few months, the whole mood of the couple had changed: she shared in her husband's social activities, and went to meetings and refresher courses. She is now happily involved with the local library. In one of our last conversations, she told me:

'That experience did me a lot of good. It forced me to abandon my attitude of the perpetual small girl in search of an image to reassure me and for me to look up to. I had no father. He used to drink and beat my mother. I hated him: I left home at sixteen to work as a domestic servant. At nineteen I married a man ten years older than I was. We quickly had three children. I didn't entirely want them, because I wasn't prepared to assume such responsibility so quickly. I have the impression of having matured and having rediscovered my husband.'

Now she seems to me to be totally liberated. She has no difficulty in inviting her ex-lover to dinner and to see the activities which she shares with her husband.

A woman of about forty came to ask my advice. Her son, a third-year pupil in a religious school, had been seduced by a literature teacher, a homosexual. Several of his fellow-pupils were in the same position. One of them eventually told his parents. They immediately went to see the Superior and the teacher was dismissed. Some days later, the parents of the pupils concerned met and decided to make a formal complaint so that this teacher should not continue his practices in another establishment. The Superior was opposed to this approach. 'You are going to make what has happened official, and that will cause a scandal. Do not forget the words of Christ, "Woe to those by whom scandal should come to pass." '

I've quoted this story because it is the same sin against the spirit. To accuse a teacher in a religious school of homosexuality is to damage the reputation of this institution. Any sensible person will see that the most important thing is to prevent a teacher who seduces boys from perverting other adolescents. To obey to the letter is to avoid making the scandal 'official'. Obeying in the spirit is accepting the consequences of the truth and protecting young people as well as possible, even those who are not part of the institution. It is true that in order to have a clear conscience you only need to make others feel guilty.

A solicitor from the sixteenth arrondissement of Paris came to see me with his seventeen-year-old daughter: she was pregnant by a Portuguese student.

'Doctor, I've brought Sylvie so that you can decide whether she should have an abortion.'

'I'm not quite sure what role you want me to play.'

'It's impossible for her keep this child.'

'Why? Was she raped?'

'No, but she will ruin her life.'

'Why?'

'Everyone will turn their back on her.'

'But it seems to me that you've brought her up in the best circles.'

'Yes, it's incomprehensible that she should have done this to us with such a good education.'

'What kind of education?'

'A religious education, given by remarkable sisters.'

'Who looked after her sexual education?'

'The sisters, of course.'

'Perhaps her mother knows (I turned to the mother, who was very embarrassed, and sitting in silence). If you will allow me, I would like to see Sylvie alone.'

I sent her parents out.

'Now, Sylvie, tell me what happened.'

'It's simple. I love this boy. One evening, after a surprise party, we were more than usually loving to each other. We made physical love. He knew all about it. I didn't know much. People never talk about that kind of thing at home.'

'And at school?'

'Not there, either. They simply warned us not to look at boys. If a boy waited for a girl at the exit, the girl was punished.'

'What do you want to do?'

'I want to keep my child. The father wants to marry me.'

'Well, I can't see any problem.'

'He's Portuguese, and he hasn't done his military service.'

'All these reasons seem inadequate to me. Stay there, I'll bring your parents back.'

(The father and mother came into my study, somewhat apprehensive.)

'Sylvie wants to keep the child and marry this boy. That seems clear.'

'But, doctor,' exclaimed the father, absolutely furious, 'you haven't worked things out: we shall never be able to marry off her sisters.'

'They will make excellent nuns.'

I learned, some months later, that this good Christian family had arranged everything in its own way, in Switzerland. I believe that they continue to go to mass regularly and with a good conscience. It is unthinkable that a Christian family which has daughters educated in religious schools should have an unmarried mother. In the face of such a scandal, abortion does not pose any problems.

This story reminds me of the advice which a nun gave to one of my colleagues who had made one of her nurses pregnant. 'I forbid you to see this child again; he is the fruit of sin. Give some money to the woman and break with her completely. You must not see either the mother or the child again.'

In connection with abortion, it is interesting to recall the position defended in *Les Etudes* (a monthly review, founded in 1856, by the Fathers of the Company of Jesus). I quote:

> As for us, we think that there is room for a distinction between human life and humanized life, and that if the individual is truly humanized only in relationship to others, by and for others, if he receives his own being from others, then the relationship of recognition, as we have outlined it, is revelatory, if not the beginning of the fully human character of the being in gestation. In other words, just as the human being does not exist without a body, so, he is not humanized without this relationship to others.'

This text is remarkable; it ends up making the divine commandment 'Thou shalt not kill' and abortion compatible. This very Jesuitical distinction between human and humanized life is a means of reconciling abortion with a good Christian conscience.

In this text, we once again come across the legalistic obsession: how to obey the letter of the law and permit abortion officially: every day young people and women die or are incapacitated as a result of clandestine abortions. Abortion must be made legal. I'm speaking about the 'legalization' of abortion by the church and not by lay authority. To obey in the spirit is to help those who are most at a disadvantage, those who cannot have an abortion in certain countries. Rather than look for the means to have a good conscience, the church as an institution should reflect on the sexual education of the younger generation.

Thanks to confession, which permits reconciliation with God, and a good conscience, which permits reconciliation with oneself, the legalistic Christian can survive. Furthermore, this attitude is comprehensible: the Christian institutions are forces of repression and resistance to change, despite some demagogic declarations which do not reflect a profound change of spirit on the part of the hierarchy. The Pope spends most of his time defending moral behaviour and discipline. He fights against birth control, divorce and the marriage of priests. Roman documents refer to the 'natural law'. The idea of the natural law comes to us from Aristotle and not from Jesus Christ. Responsible parenthood, marriage which is not a prison, celibacy freely chosen by priests who want it, and the system collapses: the laity again become free and responsible beings.

I often see priests who cannot bear celibacy. They feel as though they are treated as children, as though part of their humanity has been amputated. The fact that there is no way out of a neurotic situation makes it intolerable. If the Roman authorities relaxed their attitude and allowed the marriage of priests (if necessary, after a study of each particular case), they would create an open situation. Many priests would not marry anyway, but they would have a choice to make, as free and responsible people. Some days ago I received this letter from a priest:

> Dear Doctor,
> I am sleeping less and less, and have nightmares about having another breakdown. I want to stand up completely by myself and can't. I'm in the middle of a crowd, yet alone. I can no longer bear celibacy, and there are moments when I'm on the verge of going mad about it. For want of sleeping with a wife . . . if I could sleep with a concubine, that would do. There are days when I still have a touch of humour, and that's what gives me the courage to write to you today. Excuse me for making use of you. I so much want to be strong. I've again had bouts of crying, and you've already saved me from one.

Prohibitions connected with celibacy, contraception or abortion all represent the same more or less conscious fear: will a free man, accustomed to reflect and make his own decisions, remain in the bosom of the traditional church?

Once a prohibition is lifted, reflection is possible. Twenty years ago, well before the laws on abortion were passed, I often saw women panic-stricken as the result of an unexpected pregnancy. It was enough to begin the conversation with an open attitude for their panic to subside.

'If you want, you can have an abortion with no ethical or medical problems, and no difficulties over money. The problem isn't there. Let's think together about why you don't want to keep this child.'

I can claim that with this attitude I've prevented seventy to eighty per cent of these women from having an abortion.

The problem of divorce is very similar. Prohibition can make marriage into a situation which produces neuroses. True, Jesus exalted the love of man and women 'who are no longer two, but one flesh', and wanted this to be definitive. But, for the Christian, the most sacred law is at the service of mankind and must not become a prison from which some would love to escape at any price. There again, reflection and time are indispensable. Once more, is it necessary that the Christians concerned should have the impression that there is no other solution?

As Olivier Clement, an Orthodox theologian, recalls:

> The Eastern Church, in its great mercy, allows, or rather affirms, that a man and a woman do not always correspond to this possibility of unity in Christ which the sacrament of marriage has offered them. So it allows divorce and the remarriage of divorced persons, and welcomes broken lives into its communion.

Christian morality today is far removed from the initial message, steeped in responsibility and freedom. Charles Maurras discovered the subversive character of the gospels and blamed the ecclesiastical apparatus for having damped down this ferment. The message of Christ attacks established morality. 'The worker at the eleventh hour earns as much as those who have been working since the morning. The prodigal son who has wasted all his money on women is fêted more than the oldest son who has remained faithful to his father. Christ even says, 'The prostitutes will go before you into the kingdom of heaven.' 'Scandal and folly,' said St Paul of Christianity. 'Launch out,' said Jesus to the timid. How does one get out of the dilemma posed on the one hand by this subversive message and on the other by the rigour of an education based on prohibitions and taboos? A number of Christians remain caught between their education, which makes them infantile, and their own desires, their libido in the Freudian sense of the term, that is to say, their true sentiments, their drives and their vital instincts. It is difficult to strike a compromise, and they are incapable of maturing and becoming autonomous and responsible. . . Fortunately. . . If things were otherwise, they would be in perpetual revolt against the established order. The good conscience which they have allows them to live at peace in a society which is Christian only in name. To catechize is not to evangelize. Jean-Claude Barrault, child in an atheist family, discovered Christ at the age of eighteen:

> Great was my surprise to discover the degree to which the young Christians of my age were over-catechized but not evangelized. Catholic schools have long been considered indispensable to the church. . . Now, however, the utter failure of this policy should be recognized. I am not questioning the strictly scholarly quality of the teaching. I do denounce its habitual inability to communicate the faith. The regime of compulsory masses and courses of religious instruction has built up generations of anti-clerics or worse, clerics who confuse Christianity with a kind of morality, a kind of culture, a certain order.

> This confusion also has its good side. It prevents Christians from putting capitalist society to fire and the sword. That is one of the by no means negligible advantages of the good conscience.

3

Christian Education: its Foundations and its Human and Social Consequences

Christian education is based essentially on anxiety and fear, lack of confidence in human nature, and scorn for the body, sexuality, and woman as a sexual being.

At a very early stage, it encourages a fear of sin, and more particularly the fear of mortal sin: a child of seven cried himself to sleep every night without his parents understanding why. One day, amidst his tears, he told his father, 'I've committed a mortal sin, I said fuck to God.' The explanation was simple. His sister, aged nine, was going to catechism classes and used her new knowledge with very obvious intent. The image of a coercive God allowed her to dominate the situation and get whatever she wanted out of her small brother. Exasperated, the boy ended up by saying to her, 'Fuck God.'

I personally remember how we were prepared for first communion. We were taught how to let the host melt in our mouths, without breaking it. On my first communion I had great difficulty in dislodging the host, which became fixed to my palate. It would not melt. I had the greatest problem in keeping it from coming into contact with my teeth. Breaking the body of the Lord was a sin.

Preparation for confession was another agonizing aspect of this education. We were taught to go over our consciences with a fine toothcomb to search out the least little sin. I went to the communion table mulling over everything that I had told the priest, looking for something that I might have forgotten which could transform this communion into a sin. One of my friends, a priest, explained to me the difficulty he had in freeing himself from an anxiety which had been borne in on him during his study at minor seminary: he had a permanent worry lest impure images might cross his mind. For years he had not dared to look at a woman. The hierarchy of values he had learned among the ranks of Christian schools was as follows: do not smoke, do not play cards in school-time, work well, do not lie, do not be a bad pupil, and so on. Absolute obedience was one of the major qualities. When the bell rang, they had to stop writing immediately; if need be, leaving a word unfinished. In the evening, in the dormitory, it was forbidden to go to bed before the clock had rung. The superior set the example: he stood in his pyjamas at the foot of his bed, at attention, and then lay down as the clock struck. The chief punishment was to remain on one's knees, in the middle of the refectory, during lunch or dinner.

This priest was very calm and very gentle. He had come to consult me over a stomach ulcer, and I had great difficulty in getting him to see his problems. Progressively, he discovered that he was expending considerable energy in inhibiting all aggression in himself, so that he could apparently be at peace with everyone. He had the greatest difficulty in assuming his functions as senior priest and imposing his authority on the young priests in his charge. As a result of his apparent passivity, which his stomach was finding difficulty in tolerating, he had allowed the development, at the heart of his parish, of a particularly complicated situation: one priest had formed a group of anti-integralists, and another a group of integralists. All through the year, these two groups were in confrontation, blocking all the activities of the parish: the integralist mass was on Sunday at 9 and the anti-integralist mass at 11. The senior priest was going from bad to worse: he was receiving the representatives of one group or the other alternately up to the day when his ulcer perforated.

After an operation, this priest accepted psychotherapy, which helped him to discover the point at which his personality had been suppressed by an education based on repression and submission. He had stood his own up to the fourth-year class. To that point, without a great deal of effort, he was top of the form. At the end of the third term he was summoned into the superior's office to be told: 'You are top of your form. That is good. But your teachers' reports show that you are not working hard enough. You are profiting from your ability. Furthermore, during the year, you have broken several disciplinary rules. You will not be named top of the form on speech day; you will be third. That will teach you humility.'

For the next four successive years the young seminarian was deliberately bottom of the form. Despite that, he passed his leaving examination without any problems and went to the major seminary. Interested in philosophy and theology, he very soon regained his place at the top of the form. However, he could not help having a bad conscience, and he compensated for his academic success by a submissive attitude and a bad digestion . . . until the day when the physical symptoms no longer allowed him to bear his neurosis.

Lack of confidence in human nature is another characteristic of Christian education. In my hospital consultancy I saw a young man of eighteen, who was preparing for college. He was a boarder at a private school with a very high reputation. With surprise I learned that he was unable to work with his friends because they were forbidden to go into one another's rooms. I telephoned the headmaster, whom I knew, and asked the reasons for this attitude. He told me, 'You cannot imagine what they are capable of doing if they are allowed to meet without supervision.' As I put pressure on the headmaster, I got the reply I had expected: 'There are serious risks of homosexuality.' The same headmaster told me, 'Above all you mustn't tell young people to love one another now. They do that all too much as it is.'

My clinical experience allows me to come to quite different conclusions: far from loving themselves too much, young people cannot or do not know how to love themselves truly. Among the majority of difficult children, unhappy adolescents, couples in conflict, one always finds a lack of confidence and self-love. The aim of education is to allow children and adolescents to gain experience in security. From this perspective, lack of confidence in the educators is catastrophic, above all when the teacher projects his own fantasies which he has inherited from a pathogenic education. The headmaster whom I mentioned still projected his personal fantasies on to adolescents and thus risked inducing in them an attitude of doubt and anxiety which could damage their sexual development. Lack of psychological training among a number of teachers and the great majority of priests explain why they confuse demagogy and confidence. I know a private institution where, two years ago, the word 'compulsory' was banned. Freud himself explains how prohibitions and the limitation of pleasure are necessary for academic attainment and social and cultural advancement. In his book *Psychoanalysis of the Total Personality*, Alexander has rightly brought out the two principal types of pathogenic pedagogical methods, excessive severity and a tendency to spoil the child.

Scorn for the body, sexuality and women as a sexual being also bears witness to a lack of psychological training. If psychoanalysis can be denied the value of a therapy, it must be credited with the great achievement of having illuminated the emotional development of the child and the adolescent. Emotion and sexuality are profoundly linked. When I hear educationalists, whether or not they are priests, deny the importance of psycho-analytic training, I compare them with mountain guides smitten with blindness. From its first feed, the child discovers pleasure, its body, that of another. Its awareness of its own individuality develops through its emotional relationship with its mother. The psychological functions which ensure the conservation of the species direct pleasure towards three essential erogenous zones, the mouth, the anal sphincter and the genital organs. The three classical stages of Freudian sexuality correspond with these three zones: the oral phase, the anal phase and the phallic or genital phase. The degree to which the attitude of parents or teachers allows the child to have a complete experience of the pleasure inherent in each phase governs the risk of regression. The child may retain a particular type of behaviour, and this has allowed psychoanalysts, following Freud's example, to define oral, anal and genital characters. They contrast with the greed and dependence of orality the stubbornness, the moderation and the economy inherent in anality.

The activity which determines each stage, incorporation in the oral stage, retention or elimination in the anal stage, defines a mode of relationship with the objects of the external world, which can be transferred to other mental or physical activities, and constitutes a form of model or imaginary point of reference for them. From about the third year on, the zone of pleasure moves. The child, the education of whose sphincter is complete, concentrates its libido on its external genital organs. Erection and masturbation begin or develop. At this stage the child becomes aware of the difference between the sexes and accepts the definitive notion of its individuality in relation to the external world and elsewhere.

It is striking to note that a number of priests have not come to the end of their psychological development. Many of them have not yet resolved their Oedipus complex (see above, p. 18, and p. 167 n. 1). Granted, they are not the only ones; a number of lay people are in the same state. Parents who are too authoritarian, and forbid a child to play with its genitals or ask questions about sex, risk provoking in the child a guilt feeling which prevents it from satisfying its curiosity in the sexual sphere and sometimes hinders its growth at an emotional and psychological level. Later, the child comes to identify with its father or a paternal substitute and adopts manly and combative attitudes.

This period of adolescence is often difficult to understand. It is made up of aggression, hate and love all at once, and the child has to find a 'man to talk to'. Many priests had dominating mothers and more or less nonentities as fathers. Some of them live their whole life with a mother or a substitute mother and thus remain in a situation of filial dependence; a priest of about fifty with whom I had dined suddenly got up and said, 'I promised my mother to be home before midnight. I must leave immediately.'

Some priests who are apparently 'free' are in fact dependent on a number of old ladies with jobs in the parish who look after them jealously, and often aggressively, preventing them from having other relationships with women. These situations are frequently to be found at the start of psychological dramas and rivalries, which are often latent, and then sometimes burst out into the full light of day: two old ladies of good standing called each other 'whore' and 'slut' as they came out of the eleven o'clock mass. Priests have often come to me in a great state of anxiety, guilty at their late discovery of masturbation: two of them particularly struck me by their intellectual and cultural level and the important responsibilities which they had as teachers. The first, aged about forty, had fallen in love with a young nun with whom he had been to a teachers training college. He had had erotic dreams and painful erections which had woken him up. Clinical examination revealed a particularly tight phimosis, that is to say a long and narrow foreskin, which explained the very sharp pains caused by erection and ejaculation. He was very relieved by the anatomical and physiological explanations which I gave him. He agreed to have an operation, and then came back to see me for several therapeutic conversations. His education had been limited to rigorous prohibitions which had completely inhibited his sexual growth: three had made a particular mark on him: not to eat sugar, not to dirty himself and not to be brutal. As for the psychological significance of masturbation, he had never heard of it!

I could only keep up with this priest for a few weeks, for two reasons, the first being distance (he lived nearly two hundred miles away). The second, far more important, was that he did not really feel the need. Overwhelmed with his activities and his responsibilities, he did not seem very preoccupied with his psychological development. He had obtained 'permission' from his superior in the hierarchy to keep writing to this young nun. . . From time to time he sends me a few friendly lines, but he no longer tells me about his problem.

A priest of fifty-eight came to consult me for an identical problem, this time because he had not fallen in love. He had discovered masturbation, following nocturnal imaginings of which he could not rid himself. His guilt was increased by the recollection of the numerous seminarians whom he had condemned. He was reassured to learn that he was simply the victim of a late hyper-functioning of the sexual glands, the physiological explanation of the famous noontide demon. I told him, 'It's the swan song of your testicles. . .' This expression reassured him completely. In a few weeks, a brief course of sedative treatment removed all the problems.

Guilt-feelings about sex are particularly flagrant in good Christian families, where pre-marital pregnancy produces real dramas. The father gets angry and does not understand why 'his daughter has done this to him'. A social solution is demanded without delay: marriage or abortion. The second solution is chosen more often. The interested party is not allowed to have much say. I remember a mother who had a depression after her daughter's abortion. 'I will be punished,' she told me; 'God cannot accept that sort of thing. I am responsible and I will have to pay. I prefer it to be me.' Her daughter had retained feelings of guilt, and some years after the 'drama', now married, she was afraid of becoming pregnant because she was afraid of having abnormal children. This story is fairly characteristic: the daughter was treated as an object by her mother, and her mother thought she was being treated as an object by God; the victim of an education which retarded her, she could not bear the pregnancy of her daughter and forced her to have an abortion. Mother and daughter were now waiting for 'just punishment for their sins'.

The consequence of traditional Christian education is considerable immaturity: a number of priests cannot communicate with themselves. Some regard psychotherapy as dangerous manipulation. One has the impression that they are afraid that excessive introspection might harm their vocation. Digestive troubles are particularly frequent among priests, as among all neurotics who do not express their anxieties: however, if one compares them with a group of sick people of the same cultural level and with the same kind of symptoms, it is more difficult to get them to have psychotherapy. Everything happens as though their position as 'pastor of the flock' prevented them from getting involved in their own problems. They accept organic illness easily, but they find it hard to recognize that their physical symptoms are due to the conversion of an anxiety which has not been recognized and externalized. Thus, a priest spent the greater part of his time helping not only laity, but also some of his colleagues, to see themselves clearly. Without previous symptoms, he had a very serious gastric haemorrhage which made it necessary for him to go into hospital immediately. The X-rays showed a duodenal ulcer. After two weeks of intensive treatment and transfusion, his red blood cell count was restored from 1,800,000 to 4,500,000 and stayed there. In agreement with the surgeon, it was decided not to operate and to give him medical treatment, watching him particularly carefully. This priest was so tense and anxious that I suggested psychotherapy. From the first conversation, the block was total. 'I have no problem. My ulcer is digestive in origin and I know why: there were problems when I was weaned and I've never been able to digest cow's milk.'

In fact, attitudes of this kind are based on the primordial difficulty for which Christian education is responsible: the difficulty of loving and accepting oneself. In this way it builds up fragile superegos which are simply the internalization of a rigid and coercive external law. 'The traditional Christian' is built up from outside and not from inside. The law, under its most negative form, is represented by prohibitions and taboos. It is a matter of applying the rules without explanation or justification. The morality of 'what is allowed and what is forbidden' makes human sexuality a guilty sexuality and not a responsible sexuality. It is shown to be completely ineffective.

Paul VI seems to have complained of the treason of the Latin countries: the Italian law on divorce and the French law on abortion. He did not understand that if you shut all the stop cocks on a boiler, sooner or later you get an explosion. I wish that he could have had some experience of psychoanalysis which would have enabled him to understand the structures of the personality and the importance of an intelligent education.

According to Freud's final views, the personality is made up of three elements. The id constitutes the driving-force of the personality: its contents, the psychological expression of drives, are unconscious, in part hereditary and innate, and otherwise repressed and acquired: this is the first reservoir of psychic energy.

The ego is a psychological authority which progressively affirms itself between the id and the external world. It progressively takes on a shape of its own, recognizing itself through its perceptions, and discerning itself by becoming aware of reality. The ego is set between the forces emanating from the id and external constraints. It is the place where the drives are confronted with the reality principle, and takes over the control of direction essential for the achievement of any aim.

The ego is essentially conscious, but it is also made up of preconscious elements, which can be mobilized at will, and unconscious elements, those which it has repressed when experiences or confrontation between the id and the real have seemed to be intolerable and irreducible. The mechanism of repression prevents integration in the ego and makes it the principal victim of the blind opposition which it has directed against the id. Repression appears as an attempt on the part of the ego to escape: it gives up its directive role and its task of the construction of the personality by the mastery of the elements of the id. It is the excessive form of the process of control, and this excess is a weakness: for the ego, one part of the id remains forbidden ground.

A third force, summoned up by the very development of the personality, gradually involves itself in the relations of the ego and the id: this is the ideal ego, or superego. The superego is a superior authority, unconsciously developed by the ego as a result of its experiences. Its sources go back to the earliest periods of the formation of the personality. It is developed by the internalization of the demands of the subject's surroundings and parental prohibitions, and by identification with the persons who have served as its model. It is capable of bringing powerful forces under the control of the ego, but it is also capable of repressing them, preventing them from finding any way out, and depriving the personality of material essential for its construction. The quality of education has a decisive influence on the constitution of the superego. If the experience undergone ends up with the formation of a superego with no coercive character, a harmonious synthesis of the personality will be possible. If the opposite happens, the rigidity of the superego will lead to maladjustment: opposing itself to the progressive integration of the forces of the id, it will produce a neurotic misdirection of their energy.

If the drives come up against the veto of the ego and the prohibitions of the superego, they cannot find direct satisfactions. They look for other ways out, perhaps through regression, by the return of the libido to certain earlier phases of its development (narcissim would be a return to the autoerotic phase, and adult homosexuality a regression to the homoerotic phase), or in modes of expression sufficiently disguised for the ego to accept them and allow them to pass. It is this disguise which constitutes the symptom of the neurosis, which apparently has no connection with the initial drive. There are many manifestations of the repressed libido; phobias which are irrational, obsessive, agonized fears, like agoraphobia, a morbid fear of open places; claustrophobia, fear of being shut up: ereuthophobia, fear of blushing, and so on. Then there are *obsessional rites*, characterized by a series of actions which the subject feels obliged to perform on pain of having a feeling of unbearable anxiety. Or, more simply, there can be various physical symptoms which can even become organic – stomach aches, gastritis, stomach ulcers, colic spasms, acute or chronic colitis, problems with the heart, the skin or with breathing, not to mention impotence and neurotic asthenia, giving evidence of a blockage of psychological energy.

Freud gave a very good definition of 'normal behaviour'. What is considered correct is all attitudes of the ego which satisfy at the same time the demands of the id, the superego and reality. That happens when the ego succeeds in reconciling these different demands. We postulate that the ego sees itself obliged to satisfy at the same time both the demands of reality and those of the id and the superego, while preserving its own organization and autonomy. Only a relative or total weakening of the ego can prevent it from realizing its tasks and in so doing create possibilities for morbid states. If the two other authorities, the id and the superego, become too powerful, they succeed in disorganizing and modifying the ego in such a way that relations with reality are embarrassed, even abolished.

In fact, the ego only constructs and strengthens itself by measuring itself and adapting to the outside world, the resistance of which it experiences, and by achieving a successful resolution of the conflicts between what have been called the pleasure principle and the reality principle. This adjustment of the pleasure principle to the reality principle is absolutely necessary for our equilibrium. This equilibrium depends on a 'self-regulation' which is incompatible with systematic repression and coercion. It is a permanent dialectic between impulse and reason, instinct and spirit, constraint and liberty. Thanks to this regulation of instinctual drives, the libido finds beyond the principle of initial pleasure a pleasure of a superior quality: the brute facts of instinct are 'refined', so that pleasure is no longer the simple satisfaction of a biological need. Growth does not take place by refusing external constraints, but by accepting the constraints which the individual imposes on himself with reference to others with whom he must live, one depending on the other for their personal happiness. Education must teach people to harmonize the facts and their instincts, those of their particular situation and the collectivity to which they belong, at every moment of time. These facts change continually in the course of individual and collective history. The adult state would seem to be made up of such a faculty of permanent harmonization. It has been said that psychologically and physiologically, man is perpetually walking on a tight-rope.

How does one maintain an equilibrium of this kind while being educated in a legalistic relativization to norms external to ourselves, under the eye of a God who loves us but who, at the hour of judgment, will ask an account of us? The anguish of sin, lack of confidence in our own nature, scorn of our body and its instincts, construct a neurotic superego which is an opaque screen, inhibiting all personal creativity, making real relations with others impossible, and preventing the subject from discovering other people in all their profundity, their individual destiny and their irreducible spontaneity. The other person is there only to respond to our needs and to support our illusions.

By the education which it dispenses, the church is partly responsible for the inhuman society in which we live. Through inhibition, repression and anxiety it creates adults who are tense, unsatisfied and guilt-ridden, incapable of loving and accepting themselves. Much anti-social behaviour or behaviour which is simply damaging to the good balance of the group is the result of a sexuality which is badly integrated or unbalanced. The bourgeois, in the pejorative sense of the term, dominated by his avaricious and conservative tendencies, may be regarded as a constipated person who has remained at the anal phase of autoeroticism. Anarchism may be said to be more or less bound up with sexual obsession. Some revolutionary phenomena might be collective phenomena of the repression of an unresolved Oedipus complex: society is a collective representation of the father, and in every revolution there is an unconscious desire to murder the father. . . One fact seems significant: during the revolution of May 1968, many people were confined for secondary mental troubles with feelings of guilt following the murder of the Father. A repressive society is in fact simply the reflection of a repressive education, ending up in a profound inadequacy of the ego.

Patients have often asked whether I believe in the Devil, and whether I think Satan is a person. . . I'm very careful about answering such questions. I believe simply that God is love, sharing, communication and respect of the other, and that Satan is the symbol of repression, anxiety, hate and scorn. Why should God force people who hate each other to live together, refusing them the solution of divorce? Why should God allow women to die of abortions performed anywhere, by anyone? A practising Catholic gynaecologist agreed to do 'justified' abortions only on condition that they were performed without any anaesthetic!

The aim of Christian education should be the happiness and the psychological blossoming of the person. It is now time that, just as priests have abandoned their black soutane, a symbol of mourning, we should abandon our obsessions with death and anxiety, to live henceforth the joy of the resurrection.

I know only one definition of happiness: 'To be a good companion to oneself'. It is the only way of being a good companion to others, and of loving our neighbour as ourselves.

4

Sickness and Guilt in Christian Theology

Many apparently organic illnesses, of the kind that I have described in my two previous books,[7] are in fact conversion symptoms due to the introversion of anxiety and aggression. They coincide with critical episodes in the personal life of the patient. In part they derive from an active and unconscious elaboration, their symptoms being susceptible of interpretation in the light of depth psychology. Psychological analysis very frequently discovers guilt feelings in the most varied neuroses and in crises of personal existence. So it is normal that medical research should pose very clearly the problem of the relationship between illness and sin.

It seems that the Alexandrian and Cappadocian fathers (especially St Athanasius and St Gregory of Nyssa) were the first to develop a theological doctrine of illness. They reflected on the consequences of original sin for human nature: man created by God in his image and likeness, according to Genesis, is the image of God, but he has his own nature, human nature. If God is absolutely impassible and beyond the reach of sin, how can man, his image, be sick? The reply of St Athanasius and St Gregory of Nyssa is the same: the nature of man became susceptible to sickness because of the first sin. 'Man should have been created in a state of impassibility and asexuality.'

St Athanasius writes: 'The first objective of God was that men should not be born by marriage and corruption, but the transgression of his commandment led to sexual union because of the sin of Adam.' The bishop of Nyssa is even more explicit: 'This division into sexes in no way concerns the divine archetype. It makes human beings near to becoming irrational beings.' That in fact means that man is no longer a pure spirit, made in the image of God, but has become a being subject to his impulses. Man, as divine image, was by nature asexual and beyond the reach of illness. Without the first sin, his reproduction would be like that of 'angelic nature'. In a second stage, God, foreseeing the sin which man would commit of his own free will, added to the image the distinction of sexes. This change in human nature made it a sexual and mortal nature, capable of suffering illness. It is in this way that Gregory of Nyssa can say that the creator of sickness and death was man himself.

A theological doctrine of illness cannot be reduced to the problems of its origin: at the same time it must give an answer to the question of its significance in the economy of creation, and this significance is closely tied up with that of two other accidents of human existence: evil and pain. The answer is given us in the gospel: sin is a test and an occasion for merit. As St Basil puts it: the just accept illness like an athlete in a contest, expecting great rewards as a fruit of their patience. He expresses his idea in a letter written to Hilarius: In your bodily infirmity, I exhort you to act courageously, and as is fitting before the God who has called us: for if he sees us receiving present circumstances with thanksgiving, either he will calm our pains and our emotions, or he will give a magnificent recompense for our patience in the life to come.'

Did Christ claim that physical illness can be due in certain instances to the sins of the sick person? There are two interesting cases, that of the paralysed man in Capernaum and that of the man by the pool of Bethesda. The former is recounted by St Luke, St Mark and St Matthew.

When they could not get near him because of the crowd, they removed the roof above him; and when they had made an opening, they let down the pallet on which the paralytic lay. And when Jesus saw their faith, he said to the paralytic, 'My son, your sins are forgiven.' Now some of the scribes were sitting there, questioning in their hearts, 'Why does this man speak thus? It is blasphemy! Who can forgive sins but God alone?' And immediately Jesus, perceiving in his spirit that they thus questioned within themselves, said to them, 'Why do you thus question in your hearts? Which is easier, to say to the paralytic, "Your sins are forgiven," or to say, "Rise, take up your bed and walk"?' But that you may know that the Son of man has authority on earth to forgive sins – he said to the paralytic – I say to you, rise, take up your pallet and go home. And he rose and immediately took up the pallet and went out before them all; so that they were all amazed and glorified God.

The case of the sick man cured by the pool reflects the same attitude. Jesus cures him and says, 'Do not sin again, lest something worse happen to you.'

In my view, these two examples show that Christ thought there was a connection between sickness and sin. Jesus first suppressed the fundamental ill, sin, and then its sequel, illness.

It is important to note that in several texts of the gospels it seems that Jesus does not consider that sickness is directly the consequence of sin. It is worth recalling the text in John about the man blind since birth.

As he passed by, he saw a man blind from his birth. His disciples asked him, 'Rabbi, who sinned, this man or his parents, that he was born blind?' Jesus answered, 'It was not that this man sinned, or his parents, but that the works of God might be made manifest in him.'

The disciples, following the current view among their people, attributed physical infirmity to a sin of the sick man himself or his parents. They regarded illness as a consequence of a sin, and therefore capable of being transmitted by heredity. In his reply Jesus distinguishes two problems: the cause of the illness and its significance. He says clearly that this physical illness is not the consequence of a sin, but is 'so that the works of God might be made manifest in him'.

So man can fall ill without having sinned. Poor Lazarus is just, and he is covered with sores which the dogs come to lick. It is in connection with the sickness of Lazarus that Jesus says, 'This sickness does not lead to death, but to the glory of God, so that the son of God may be glorified by it.' So it is that in the eyes of Christians, every illness has a second significance: it is a spiritual test of the sick person to give the person a chance of merit. The attitude of Christ is very different from that of Plato, who in his *Phaedrus* speaks 'of illnesses and other terrible tests which, as a result of ancient offences, and without one knowing whence they come, afflict certain families'.

Some Christians regard their illness truly as a test sent by God, while co-operating with the doctor to cure it as quickly as possible. Others, on the other hand, remain passive, like this young woman afflicted with multiple sclerosis.

At our first meeting, she told me, 'God tries those whom he loves. He will cure me if he wants to.' This disease develops progressively, in stages sometimes several years apart, and our therapeutic action is still very limited. At each remission, the patient thanked God. At each new stage she glorified him. All those around her regarded her as a saint. On Sunday she took communion in the parish where I went to mass. Before the Christian congregation, supported by her husband, she went down the church with her eyes fixed on the cross. I have never seen a multiple sclerosis develop so rapidly. In a few months, the patient was bed-ridden. I admitted her to the Salpetrière Hospital several times. She took everything without a complaint and spent her days in prayer. She died of lack of nutrition and exhaustion. Her family doctor, the physiotherapist and I were all convinced that she had allowed herself to die, happy to suffer for the greater glory of God.

Catholic theology seems to be forced to a conclusion: human sickness, thanks to the divine gift, did not exist in the state of original justice which preceded the first sin. It appeared on earth as a consequence of this original sin. The physical consequences of the loss of original perfection were death, sickness and pain. If Adam and Eve had not violated the divine law, their descendants would have grown up and developed without being subjected to pain and to ailments of the body and the spirit. As far as the soul is concerned, St Thomas distinguishes four wounds which correspond to the four cardinal virtues: ignorance, which affects reason and prudence; malice, which affects the will and justice; weakness, which affects the power to be angry and strength; and concupiscence, which affects the power of desire and temperance. To these wounds of the spirit it is necessary to add those which affect the body: death and all the physical infirmities connected with it.

Janssen, a Catholic author, wrote:

> If by suffering we understand physical transformation coming from within, as in certain illnesses, or from the outside, as in certain traumatic lesions the effect of which is to produce decay followed by death, in this case the suffering must be excluded from the state of our first parents to the same extent as death. Pain was inflicted on them as a punishment for sin: acute pain when Eve was condemned to the sufferings of childbirth, and unremitting pain when Adam was condemned to earn his bread by the sweat of his brow.

So it appears that according to Catholic theology, original sin had a threefold consequence for mankind: death, work and, for woman, the pains of childbirth. This last point seems to me important: for many women it is necessary to have pain in childbirth; that is part of the divine law.

For five years, a young woman refused to have a child. The reason for her refusal was simple: she was afraid of giving birth. Throughout her childhood and adolescence as an only daughter, she had heard her mother describe, in minutest detail, the course of her own child-bearing, ending her story by stigmatizing the attitude of all the young girls who no longer wanted to suffer and in so doing transgressed the will of God.

In psychotherapy, she discovered that in fact she detested her mother and that unconsciously she was opposed to pregnancy through a refusal to identify with her. Fear of childbirth was only the apparent expression of her aggression. After several months of treatment she was ready to become pregnant and gave birth without apprehension. The midwife was amazed at her calm and readiness to cooperate.

Her husband, who came to thank me, said with a smile, 'My wife takes a perverse pleasure in telling her mother that her child-bearing remains one of the most pleasant memories of her life.'

On the other hand, it seems that Catholic theology does not consider sickness as a direct consequence, such as the punishment of a personal sin in addition to original sin. It is enough to repeat the words of Jesus Christ in the presence of the man blind from birth: neither he nor his parents have sinned, but his sickness serves to manifest the works of God in him. This way of thinking is very different from that of the ancient Semitic peoples who attributed all their ills to personal sins. The frame of mind is part of the ancient pattern of human thought, and neither the spread of Christianity nor the progress of scientific thought have succeeded in suppressing it completely. The conviction that sickness is a direct punishment for a serious sin was very widespread in the Christian world of antiquity. More recently, Luther attributed illnesses to the devil. Sickness, he said, does not come from God, who is good and always does good; it comes from the devil, who is the source of all mishap. Even now, Christian Scientists express the same view: 'The person whose mind follows the right lines does not fall ill.' Christian theology has drawn a clear distinction between sin and sickness. In its very essence, sin is purely spiritual, but that does not mean that it is not responsible for a certain number of physical reactions. On the contrary, the physiological and psychological make-up of man requires that the body should participate in some way in all his actions, even the most spiritual of them, like an unexpressed thought or an intimate desire. However, sickness appears only if man has transgressed the divine law, and has done so freely and consciously. The clear distinction between sickness and sin does not exclude a relationship between them, not only as vicissitudes affecting the same subject, but as both representing the disorders of human existence.

St Thomas writes that actual sin deprives man of a grace which is given him to guide the operations of his soul aright, and not to preserve him from corporeal deficiencies. However, certain sins can engender pathological emotions, which is what happens to those 'who fall sick and die because they have eaten too much'.

The harmful action of sin on physical health can in any case be slow and progressive. This is the case with bad habits, which can gradually change the constitution of the person who forms them, and as a result alter the normality of his or her physical reactions. More subtly still, wrongdoing, understood in the broadest sense of the term, as a transgression of the moral law which each person accepts and recognizes as necessary, brings in its train an inexorable sequel: a feeling of guilt.

Only rarely does this state express itself in a symbolic form, giving rise to mental disorders or even changing the function of certain organs, this change of function in certain organs ultimately perhaps leading to lesions at weak points of the organism. It is by no means rare that a 'sick soul' in the moral sense ends up by becoming a sick soul in the medical sense. The guilt which cannot be assumed is translated into mental and then physical disorders. Theology establishes a close connection between the tranquillity of the soul and the health of the body. Thus, Christianity which, in contrast to the Greeks and the Semites, has taught a radical difference between sin and sickness, has established the existence of a secondary relationship.

The remarkable achievement of primitive Christianity was to overcome the opposition between thorough-going Greek naturalism and abusive Greek personalism. Primitive Christianity found a middle way between the doctrine of the Semite, who saw the sick man as a sinner, and the theory of the Greek, who had come to see the sinner as a sick man. It transposed the *raison d'être* of the two doctrines to a higher level and, without having this objective exclusively in mind, made possible a real psychosomatic pathology. However, for this possibility to be realized it would be necessary to make systematic use of a method of exploration and a therapy distinct from the sensorial exploration of the Greeks and the quantitative exploration of the moderns, i.e. that of dialogue. This only came about in the twentieth century. Whereas medicine has always been more or less psychosomatic, only in our day has it been possible to develop a pathology worthy of this name.

Christian theology has still expressed two important ideas. If actual sin is not responsible for illness, illness always appears as a trial, making it possible, if the illness is accepted, to glorify God. Suffering, in its most general sense, has a significance in the economy of creation. It is an opportunity for spiritual benefit. Suffering is borne better the further the spirit of the one who suffers has moved towards a high degree of perfection. It is a subjective and variable way of feeling and testing reality.

Doubtless a really virtuous individual and social life which takes account of the rules of prudence, justice and temperance, will not save men from all ills, but it will make their illnesses much less frequent and, in every case, much more tolerable. On the other hand, sickness offers those who suffer from it and do not accept it manifold occasions for sin. Anger, hate, despair, lying and all kinds of other violations of the divine law are often the sorry moral consequence of sickness.

It is certain that a virtuous life in the true sense of the term can be a guarantee of psychological balance and health. I have often been able to note how openness to others and true love help towards a psychosomatic balance. Unfortunately, virtue is not always understood in this sense. Often, it is a suit of armour. A certain number of Christians, 'virtuous, prudent, upright and temperate', spend their lives protecting themselves from sin and anguish, and turning in on themselves, to be preoccupied with their body and their spirit. They are very afraid of sickness and death, but do not show it. Apparently detached, under pressure from their family, they come simply to ask for a mechanical check-up.

This type of virtue is most conducive to psychosomatic illnesses, that is to say, those which are due to the retention of anxiety which is not expressed in the body.

An engineer of about fifty came to consult me for cardiac pains, which produced angina. Examination revealed blood pressure of 140/85 and a normal electro-cardiogram. From all the evidence, these troubles were nervous in origin. I carefully tried to open up a dialogue to try to understand the real causes of this lack of equilibrium.

'I think that your troubles are due to tiredness.'

'I'm not tired.'

'Do you have business or family worries?'

'No, all is going well.'

'I'm going to prescribe you a sedative to lower your tension and soothe your pains.'

'I never take drugs. Besides, I don't believe in medicine.'

'Why did you come to see me, then?'

'To please my wife.'

'All right, do as you wish. But you are still young. This hypertension and these cardiac pains may be the first signs of a heart attack. You ought to have regular check-ups.'

'Thank you, doctor.'

Polite and distant, he quickly took his leave. Some days later, his wife made an appointment. Disturbed, she came with her news.

'My husband came back from his appointment with you very troubled.'

'He refused the treatment I suggested.'

'My husband is a perfect man. His only fault is being absolute. He cannot bear anyone to disagree with him, or any change in his habits. It is unthinkable for him to be ill. He leads a regular life, and I don't think he has any vices. He doesn't drink, doesn't smoke, and follows a very strict diet.'

'I think that his troubles are due to abnormal psychological tension.'

'Ah, I understand better. The poor man has too many worries at the moment. He cannot bear the way things are going in the church. He's an integralist and is in perpetual conflict with our parish priest. The unexpected arrival of our only son, with his wife and two small children, didn't help. They came back from Africa, with no work and nowhere to live. The house is large and I didn't see any problem in inviting them to stay.'

'Your husband can't bear being disturbed?'

'He needs a calm and regular life. Our grandsons are very noisy.'

'I think that you're right. You've mentioned the real causes of his present state.'

'What shall I do, doctor?'

'Hope that your parish priest will start saying mass in Latin again and that your son leaves as soon as possible.'

Opening the door of my study, this splendid wife stopped for a moment and said to me:

'You know, doctor, he's the best of men. He has a remarkable faith.'

'I don't think, madam, that that will be enough to lower his tension.'

I never saw her husband again.

It is interesting to discover that the origin of psychosomatic medicine goes back to the Christian conception of sickness. The passions and 'guilt' can be the cause of mental and physical upsets, and therefore be factors in illness. Furthermore, resistance to sickness will depend to a great extent on the mental balance of particular subjects, on their 'virtue', the perfection of their souls. By contrast, the illness suffered can itself be a factor of sin and bring with it a diminution of the resistance of the sick person. The doctor can bring about cure of the body, but the Christian must relieve the sick person by the word and by 'the love of charity'.

The cure of patients, writes Clement of Alexandria at the beginning of the *Paidagogos*, is achieved by the Logos, exhortation. As a tranquillizing medicine, he strengthens souls by gentle prescriptions and brings sick persons to full knowledge of the truth. Thus the word brings about a spiritual conversion and a psychological cure. St Basil wrote to his physician Eustathius: 'In your case, science is ambidextrous, and you push back the accepted limits of philanthropy, not continuing the beneficial nature of your art to the body, but also securing the cure of souls.' Doctor Eustathius seems to have been skilled in psychosomatic ailments.

One could cite numerous texts vaunting the curative action of the word of Christ: 'The Logos of the Father,' writes Clement of Alexandria, 'is the only doctor who can deal with our human weakness. We call the Logos "saviour" because he has invented spiritual medicines for the well-being and salvation of mankind. He preserves health, discovers evils, diagnoses the causes of ailments, cuts the roots of unreasonable appetites, proposes a regime of life, and prescribes all the antidotes which can save us from evil.'

Alongside him, Origen writes, 'We look after ourselves by the remedy of the doctrine of faith.'

Pushing this theory to its limits, Christians began to think the use of drugs impermissible, as if one could achieve health only through prayer and exorcism. Tatian allows non-Christians to use medicine, but forbids Christians to do so:

In all instances, medicinal cure derives from deceit, for if anyone is cured by his confidence in the properties of matter, he will be cured all the more by abandoning himself to the power of God. If someone entrusts himself to the properties of matter, why does he not entrust himself to God?

Certainly, Christians have never thought that they could cure without the aid of God. They have always had recourse to the prayer of priests and sacramental unction. In some cases it was thought that the sickness was due to demonic possession, and exorcism, always practised in the name of Christ, was used, sometimes excessively.

Little by little, on the fringe of Christianity, superstitions and pseudo-miracles appeared which are still very common in the twilight worlds of Christianity. Numerous sects have appeared, gathering together a small number of elect, persuaded of having the truth and condemning to eternal damnation those who do not join them. It is interesting to see that this marginal religiosity began as early as the first centuries of the Christian era: exorcisms, true or false relics, amulets, magical pseudo-Christian ceremonies, and so on.

Christian literature of the second and third centuries (Tertullian, Tatian, Justin) shows how the culmination of this development was exorcism in the name of Christ, with the admixture of a degree of demonology. Thus, very soon, a number of Christians, depending on their human needs, associated rites and beliefs of other religions with their faith to the point of making an informal doctrine, without theological consistency and approaching magic and imposture.

Superstition and false medical miracles have always existed in the lower twilight areas of the Christian world. It must be said in defence of Christians who still believe in magical practices, in exorcism, in amulets and medical pseudo-miracles, that the New Testament often mentions possessed people, sometimes through the very words of Christ. 'Depart from them', Jesus orders the two possessed people of Gerasa. 'Be quiet and depart from this man,' he says to the man in the synagogue possessed with an unclean spirit. There is no doubt about it. By his attitude and his words, Jesus taught that some illnesses were produced by demons or by 'unclean spirits'.

What are we to think of these cases of possession? Two attitudes are possible: either we admit the possibility of demonic possession, and the reality of the cases described in the New Testament, or we try to demonstrate that the terms possession, demon, unclean spirit are simply archaic names for some illnesses like epilepsy and hysteria.

Some years ago, Pierre Dumayet made a television programme about the magical rites used by peasants to protect their cattle, the inexplicable death of which was attributed to a demon. The parish priest readily appeared on the screen to explain that he recited prayers of exorcism and that they produced excellent results. He was more effective than the vet, and cheaper. It is interesting to note that the peasants always called the vet. If, statistically, the results obtained by the prayers of exorcism were satisfactory, they would never have needed him. Many people, whether Christians or not, look for easy solutions external to themselves, to sort out their psychological, physical or material difficulties: the use of magic is far from being the easiest and the most reassuring. Several times I have had to treat patients who were playing the doctor off against the exorcist. There is still a great exorcist in Paris who comes on request to recite prayers of exorcism and sprinkle with holy water places and people who are victims of demonic possession. Personally, I have never found his help very effective. . .

A middle-aged woman came to consult me about her daughter, who had had a nervous breakdown.

'When the least thing crosses her,' she told me, 'my daughter falls to the ground and rolls around. She writhes, tugs at her clothes and tears her hair. Then she loses consciousness.'

'How old is she?'

'Thirty-two.'

'How long has she had these symptoms?'

'Since my husband went bankrupt, ten years ago. We had a small boutique.'

'What happened?'

'My husband always bought too much. We had a very large stock. Now fashion changes so quickly. . .'

'Is your daughter single?'

'Yes, unfortunately. . . She was going to get married . . . just before my husband's bankruptcy.'

'You've had her examined?'

'Yes. We've seen at least a dozen doctors for her nerves.'

'Have you any examinations to show me?'

She brought out of a large envelope five electro-encephalograms and two brain scans. I examined them carefully.

'These are all normal.'

'Then why does she have these spells? We think that she's possessed. Our parish priest sent a religious to exorcize her.'

'What did he do?'

'He recited prayers and threw holy water in different corners of the room to drive out Satan and his demons.'

'Was the result satisfactory?'

'He's only come three times. He told us it would take a long while.'

'Do you want me to treat your daughter?'

'Can you do anything for her?'

'I think so.'

The first two sessions of psychotherapy were very painful. The 'possessed' girl stayed quiet and immobile, looking fixedly in front of her. At the third session I told her brutally,

'In fact you're furious at your father for going bankrupt. That ruined your marriage.'

She looked at me fixedly for several seconds, and then had a magnificent fit. I've never seen such a good fit of hysteria. She fell to the ground and threw herself around, her limbs stiff, her breathing spasmodic, foam on her lips. Suddenly she began to tug at her neckline as though she were choking, clawed at her face making groaning sounds, and then jerked all four limbs and stayed still, apparently unconscious. I sat at my desk and waited for the fit to end. Then I went over to check that she was not really unconscious. To do that I took off one of her shoes and bent her toes firmly. She let out a cry.

'You're nothing but a brute.'

She sat on the ground and looked at me with a furious air. I went back to my desk and waited to see what would happen next. She stayed in the same position for several minutes, then got up suddenly, came over to my desk, seized my bronze lamp and threw it violently on the floor. I didn't move, and simply said,

'A pity, that was beautiful.'

She rushed to the window, opened it and shouted:

'I'm going to commit suicide.'

'We're on the sixth floor, you'll kill yourself. At best you'll be completely paralysed.'

She suddenly turned round and said,

'You're a monster. You don't care if I do kill myself.'

She stayed still in front of the window for two or three minutes, then shut it and said, laconically, 'It's cold.'

She was exhausted, and so was I. She came back to sit down again.

'Have you a cigarette?'

I offered her a packet of Gauloises. She took one, and lit it with the lighter on my desk.

'I'd like a glass of water.'

At my request, the secretary brought her a bottle of mineral water and a glass. She drank three glasses with evident pleasure.

'Thank you, I feel better.'

Now at last she was relaxed and at ease.

'Doctor, weren't you afraid?'

'No, I've more resistance than my lamp.'

'You're the first one not to have given me an injection. After their filthy drugs I'm exhausted for two days. . . What do you want to know?'

'Nothing.'

'Doesn't my story interest you? Ask me some questions.'

'What?'

After some seconds of hesitation, she began to talk very rapidly in an angry voice.

'My parents are completely mad. They understand nothing. They drag me along from doctor to doctor, convinced that I have epileptic fits. They've even had me exorcised. They don't know what to do. My father is in despair; when I have fits, he cries. My mother tells her beads and has masses said for my cure. What an atmosphere! And it's been going on for ten years. Before, things were different: at home people talked about nothing but money; my parents were always arguing. My father was never any good at buying. He accumulated a stock of unsaleable horrors. Then one day the ceiling fell through. The bank refused to cover the overdraft and my father was forced to sell everything off. He now works at a *de luxe* Woolworth's.'

'Are there *de luxe* Woolworth's?'

She smiled, and went on in a rather less vehement tone.

'To hell with all their talk of cash. The serious thing is what they did to ruin my life. I was working for a degree in English, and I knew a boy in the faculty who was my age and working for a degree in Russian. We had decided to get married just as my father had his troubles. The real drama is to be an only daughter. My parents begged me not to get married straight away. My father told me he wanted me to make a good marriage. My mother pleaded with me, wringing her hands, and my father begged pardon, on my knees, for his unworthiness. It was a real circus. In fact he was afraid that I would leave. They were afraid of being by themselves. My fiancé would not put up with my prevarications. He forced me to choose between him and my parents. I was weak. I didn't know how to get away from the family hothouse right up to the day when my fiancé broke with me.' (She cried as she said the last words.)

'Why didn't you leave?'

'I was incapable of it. I would have felt that I was killing them. You don't know them. They think that they adore me. In fact, they've always dreamed of keeping me. They're rotten middle-class egotists. Of course, I've all I could want: hi-fi, colour television in my room, small car. I'm looked after . . . but I can't bear them any more. I earn my living as an English teacher in a private school. I could leave, but where would I go, and with whom? Now I'm the one who is afraid of being alone. I'm weak, weak, weak!'

'Is it perhaps your fits which prevent you from leaving?'

'My fits? I know why they happen. One evening, just after I broke with my fiancé, I wanted to take a bronze lamp which is on the mantelpiece in our sitting room and break their skulls with it. I felt an enormous anxiety and had the feeling that I was choking. Then I fell to the ground shouting in despair and tearing my clothes.'

'What did your parents do?'

'They called the doctor, but he didn't understand. He asked for tests.'

'So then, why do you have your fits?'

'I think it's my only way of not killing them. I'm always tense and anxious. I can't bear them to contradict me. If they do, I explode.'

Her psychotherapy lasted for more than a year. First I had individual sessions with her. Then, I got her to take part in group therapy. The problem was clear, but the more difficult thing remained to be done: to enable this young woman of thirty-two to break away from an infantile and constraining family atmosphere. At the same time, I made her join a drama group.

After the conversation which I've described, she did not have another single fit. Granted, I prescribed her quite powerful tranquillizers so that she could stand her parents. Now, all is well. She lives in an apartment quite a long way from her family home, which she left three months after beginning her treatment. She refused any more sessions of exorcism. Her parents are not completely persuaded that her cure was medical. . .

Now she is full of activity. She continues to act, she has learnt the guitar, and recently joined a university choir. I think she's completely cured.

In its conception of the relationship between sickness and sin, Christian theology has laid stress on the importance of good relations with God to maintain a person's physiological and psychological balance. Original sin subjected men to work, suffering, sickness and death. But they can avoid sickness or make it tolerable through their psychological equilibrium and their virtue. Anxiety and guilt are sometimes determinative and always aggravating.

Pedro Lain Entralgo[8] has defined what he calls the anthropological novelty of Christianity: Christ became man to preach the kingdom of God and to show us the way we are to take. This preaching presupposes a profound change in our view of man and the world. As for the conception of man, here, from the medical point of view, are the three most important innovations.

1. The explicit affirmation of the psychological and moral inwardness of the individual. 'You have heard that it was said to the men of old, "You shall not kill," but I say to you, "Whoever is angry against his brother will be brought before the court." You have heard it said, "You shall not commit adultery," but I say to you, "Whoever looks covetously on a woman has already committed adultery with her in his heart." '

2. The absolute affirmation of the other-worldliness of every human being in that God has created them in the divine image and likeness, and they are capable of becoming children of God. If by nature one understands the created world, then 'man', the natural or physical creature, is at the same time essentially a trans-natural or trans-physical creature. It is to this dimension of his being, which constitutes his ontological inwardness, that his psychological inwardness, his moral responsibility and his freedom must ultimately be attributed. It is thanks to this that every human being is not only a nature but a person.

3. The doctrine according to which the perfection of human relationships consists in the love of charity: 'This is my commandment: love one another, as I love you,' that is to say, love with a love which, in contrast to Hellenistic *eros*, the love of desire and aspiration, is a generous gift of itself, an effusion of being in a state of plenitude towards the being in a state of need or privation.

The goal of Christian education, then, should have been to make people free, responsible men, capable of knowing themselves and ready to arrive at this state of plenitude which allows the generous gift of oneself.

PART II

THE CHRISTIAN NEUROSIS
AND CIVILIZATION

5

*Is Civilization Evolving,
or in a State of Crisis?*

Our civilization has tried to fill what Abbé Oraison calls 'the fundamental gulf of being'. It searches passionately for 'well-being', and in so doing seems to confuse two notions: material comfort and happiness. These two notions are not in themselves opposed, but the second does not follow automatically from the first. Mounier said that in our Western civilization we have succeeded in obtaining all possible ways of living, but we no longer have reasons for them.

Material prosperity, the fact that we no longer need to struggle to survive physically, has shifted the problem. Now we have to struggle to survive psychologically, other than by renunciation and systematic repression.

Among my patients I have a number of youths who could be classed as hippies, some on drugs and some not. One of them, aged about nineteen, a lawyer's son, had left home more than a year ago. I had seen him before, when he was about twelve. At that time he was a difficult child, no more. Passionately interested in entomology, he had shown me all the wealth of his collection of butterflies and insects. I had had difficult relationships with his parents. The father, an integralist, had a particularly rigid moral code, the mother, somewhat overwhelmed, found her equilibrium through her parish activities (catechism and good works). I had advised them to support their son's cultural activities as much as possible and to try to involve him with other groups of young people. I did not see him after that. He arrived unexpectedly one afternoon and asked to see me as quickly as possible. I found it very difficult to recognize the twelve-year-old boy in this adult with a gaunt, bronzed face, encircled with a substantial beard. I've tried to transcribe a summary of our conversation.

'Why do you want to see me?'

'I need to talk to you.'

'Where have you come back from with that marvellous tan?'

'From Nepal. . .'

'When did you leave home?'

'About fifteen months ago.'

'What a journey!'

'I got bored. It was a moronic life. You know my family; my father far too busy, my mother rigid and demanding, and, to complete the picture, boring studies.'

'Why boring?'

'I left school at the end of the third year, because I couldn't get into the fifth year scientific stream. I don't like maths. The supervisor said, "He can go down to the literary stream." It was a disgrace for my parents not to have a budding graduate. They put me in a private school.'

'And then?'

'It was a catastrophe. The school was tolerable enough, but working to get into the fifth year scientific stream while surrounded by people obsessed with the reputation of their school and their contract with the state was sheer slavery.'

'Perhaps you're exaggerating a bit?'

'Hardly. My parents forced me to join the school scout troop. Compulsory outings, compulsory camps. The only scoutmaster who was any good left: he suggested that we should organize some canoe trips for the summer. The families were shocked.'

'Why?'

'By the real risk. As long as we're just playing games, it's all right, but when anyone talks of doing something valuable, the mothers rise up in arms and protest.'

'And the fathers?'

'They keep quiet.'

'Not all of them!'

'Mine did. At seventeen, I was not allowed to go out by myself to buy a pair of shoes. He came with me and went up to the step-ladder himself, so that I didn't see the shop-girl's legs.'

'Perhaps he was just being chivalrous?'

'You must be joking. Him chivalrous! He's just a bear. No one ever comes to our house; he has his paper, television on Sunday interspersed with Merovingian history and stamp collecting. I was bored stiff. I started to smoke pot with my friends. They lent me some books on Buddhism and Hinduism.'

'What made you decide to leave?'

'Boredom and anxiety.'

'How did your journey come about?'

'Three of us went off. We had got to know one another smoking pot: a boy who played the guitar in a club and his girl friend, and a girl of about eighteen whose parents had just got divorced.'

'Didn't your parents look for you?'

'It was in July. I left them word that I was going on holiday with friends and that we would be camping in Corsica.'

'Good organization! Did you have papers?'

'All I needed, visas and exit permits. The guitarist saw to that.'

'How did you travel?'

'Hitch-hiking.'

'You had money?'

'Yes. I sold my motor-cycle and my hi-fi. We shared everything.'

'Tell me about the journey.'

'We ended up in an apartment in Istanbul where lots of people were crammed in together. I didn't stay long. It was full of people who were injecting. They called them the junkies. We were content to smoke.'

'What does pot do for you?'

'It's incredible. All the barriers come down. No more communication problems, no more cops, no more conventions, no more anxiety; it's easy to express yourself.'

'Where did you go after Istanbul?'

'I crossed Turkey, Iran, Afghanistan, sometimes on foot, sometimes by car when a tourist gave us a lift.'

'Were there many of you?'

'About ten.'

'How did you manage for food?'

'Not very well, we ate rice. Then we smoked pot. Out there it's cheaper than food. . . We arrived in India: what a cheat! We found it a wretched world.'

'What did you do?'

'I managed to keep off injecting, otherwise that would have been it. We decided to leave for Nepal.'

'Many of you?'

'No, just the three. A lot of others left for Benares.'

'And Nepal?'

'In seventy miles you go from 300 feet to 13,000. When you leave the plain of the Ganges, and cross the Terai jungle, you find hills and cultivated terraces, the Himalayas. You go through villages with their little temples. The people are cheerful, relaxed, hospitable, women with flowers in their hair. The inhabitants of this region are very poor, but they're not unhappy. In the streets of Katmandu, you find folk singers accompanying themselves on the violin.'

'What did you do in Nepal?'

'We continued to live in a group. We stayed with others in a two-roomed Nepalese house. We managed to live on next to nothing. But we were drawn in on ourselves: the language barrier is harder to cross than mountains. I liked the atmosphere of the place very much, all the same; the thousands of temples in the valley. Prayer-wheels and hangings everywhere. There are gods for everyone.'

'Did you stay in Nepal long?'

'Four months.'

'Why did you come back?'

'There was no other solution. It is impossible to get integrated into communities of lamas. You're isolated and aimless. You have to find a community of your own.'

'How did you get back?'

'I told my father, and he got me back.'

'The return can't have been easy.'

'No, but there were no surprises. They're still as shut in as ever. You may not believe it, but they didn't ask me anything about the trip. My mother simply said, "How thin you are! You should go to the barber." My father just asked whether I had any intention of resuming my studies. I didn't reply. I came to see you because I needed to talk to someone who would listen.'

'Have you any ideas?'

'Yes, I want to become a journalist and get involved in reporting. I want to earn my living. I don't want to be a part of this collective hysteria: people working all the time and not knowing why. Then they buy something or other – it doesn't matter what; it gives them a goal in life. I don't want to study any more; I'm incapable of returning to college. I would go back, as my father puts it, by the narrow gate. As soon as I can, I would like to go back to Nepal, I'd like to see Goa, Ceylon, Laos, Thailand. I'd even like to go to Kyoto, the capital of Zen. I'd do some real reporting.'

'Do you still smoke pot?'

'A little. It's not much fun by yourself.'

This young man had made his journey. He had come back resolved to live his life as he wanted to. 'My mother,' he told me, 'keeps saying incessantly that everything comes from God. Now I'm sure that we make our own lives and that we are on our own.'

I've quoted this comment to show the point at which a number of young people who might be called drop-outs are in fact looking for meaning in life, which is difficult to find in our technological, industrial, commercial, consumer society. They are in search of communication, of sharing in small groups, or techniques of initiation, methods based on the development of the inner life, of the mystical life, coming close to religious initiation. They are in search of a new form of life and spirituality.

The development of these young people is simply the consequence of a profound modification of traditional society. The collapse of patriarchal society is an important element in this development.

The collapse of patriarchal society

The father is no longer the solemn and authoritarian patriarch, watching over his children's discipline with a firm hand. The function of the father is evolving and moving on from the period of command to that of witness. There is no longer one head of the family; there are two. Paternal power has been replaced by parental power: from now on, father and mother are on an equal footing. This is a remarkable revolution, the most remarkable, in fact, in this area in all the centuries since the time of Jesus. If we are to understand the present-day problem of fatherhood, it must be put in a much wider framework: that of the expansion and the collapse of patriarchal society. This kind of society has not always existed, nor is it the only one conceivable. Even now, in Oceania, there are societies of a matriarchal type, in which the line is that of the mother, the children being brought up by the mother and one of her brothers. The first beginnings of an agrarian civilization are directed towards the inauguration of a matriarchy. It was in fact the wives who discovered agriculture, first in the modest form of gardening, while men were out hunting. The procreative mother made the earth fertile; without her intervention, it would have remained sterile. She dominated the new agrarian society. The wife had several husbands whom she maintained and whom she used for bringing up children, educating them, and defending the villages, which were constantly threatened by non-agricultural nomads. The first agrarian society was collective. Conception was considered a divine event, by which the woman entered into magical contact with the deity, and the husband had no rights over her, her children or her lands. At the beginning of the fourth millennium, men revolted against this matriarchy, and after a long and terrible struggle the woman was dethroned on earth and in heaven: the goddesses, mothers of fertility, were supplanted by solar male deities. Man became the head of the family. His children bore his name, and property passed from the collective to the private stage. Sons, and especially the oldest son, became privileged heirs. This patriarchal order was established at every stage of society, from the peasant to the king. The king is the proprietor of the kingdom, and his subjects are his children: 'My children,' Louis XVI still said to the people of Paris when they came to Versailles to ask for bread. The patriarchal model was even established in the church: the bishop of Rome became 'the Most Holy Father', and Christians his 'very dear children'.

The industrial revolution overturned agrarian society, so it is not surprising that the patriarchal system was put in question. But it is worth noting that this questioning began before the industrial revolution. Luther dealt it the first blow, when he rebelled against the authority of the 'Holy Father'. Subsequently the Puritans, whose religious organization was very egalitarian, carried his attack further. Not only was the authority of the Pope challenged, but that of the king. The king is the father of his subjects: regicide is identified with parricide. Cromwell and the Puritans finally committed this parricide. A century afterwards, the members of the Convention did the same thing to the French king. It was the end of the hereditary monarchy and the divine right of kings. In the twentieth century, kings either fall or are relegated to an honorific position, like venerable relics of the past.

The challenge to the patriarchal model does not stop there. After the revolt against the paternal authority of the Pope, and then of the king, in the nineteenth century there was a revolt among socialist theoreticians against the divine right of the employer and private ownership of the means of production. It was in 1880 that the word 'paternalism' began to be used in a pejorative sense to describe the patriarchal or paternalistic conception of the role of the owner of a business.

Today the role of the father has become uncomfortable. Over the centuries he was able to use the support of a paternalist structure of society: he was quite naturally the mediator, that is to say, the link between his home and the outside world. Now he is no longer the sole master. Society takes his children from him at a very early age, to send them to school, which keeps them for an increasingly long period. Children are no longer considered their father's property or his employees: one of the best indications of this is the new date for a return to school in mid-September. Formerly, the date of the long holidays was calculated so that the children would be home to gather in the harvest, and they would not return to school until it had been reaped: now the father must find his manual labour outside the family.

The importance of the mass media, like radio and television, no longer needs to be demonstrated. The external world makes its mark on children before the father has been able to exercise his role as mediator. The power of the image is such that things aren't true 'because father said so', but because it was said on television.

I am amazed by the number of adolescents who come to see me without being accompanied by their parents (or at least by one of them). A boy of fifteen came to consult me in order to discover all about contraception.

'People talk a lot about it in the papers and on television. I tried to discuss it at home. My father told me it was not a matter for children.'

After I had given him all the explanations he wanted, I asked him why he was so interested in this question.

'For my own education,' he told me solemnly. 'I don't like being ill-informed.' He thanked me, paid his fee, and left, with a satisfied air.

A boy of sixteen came to ask for information about drugs. He had never taken any. He asked me about the different types which were generally used, the reactions they produced and the risks they might involve.

'I daren't ask all these question at home. They would think that I wanted to take drugs. And then, I don't think my mother and father know much about it. At school, some of my friends boast about taking drugs. They say that they've had incredible sensations. They've offered me pot to smoke. I refused. Now I can discuss it with them. I'm sure they know less than I do.'

The emancipation of women is another feature of the problem: woman has become man's equal. She does the same studies, she is a full citizen, with the vote, and can be elected mayor or deputy. Now she is equal head of the family. The new egalitarian model of authority is not yet fully established, and the husband, doubting himself and his role, can become spineless and unsure of himself, handing over virtually all the running of the family to his wife: this establishes a *de facto* matriarchy. Many women experience this situation with a feeling of guilt and frustration: 'If only my husband played his role as a father!'

All psychologists are now agreed on one point: the family must have both a masculine and a feminine pole. The child only finds a balance if there is a man with whom he can identify, in the case of the boy, or with whom it is possible to identify a man, in the case of the girl. This man is normally the mother's husband. In some cases it is another man, when there is no father, either because he is dead or because he has not married the mother.

Specialists in child psychology and pathology, like Maud Mannoni, have stressed the fact that cases of mental retardation and even psychosis could arise when the mother never speaks of the father: it is important that the mother should allow the intrusion of a third, male person into her relationship with her child, otherwise the child is shut up in a dual situation with its mother, and this situation does not allow it to find its autonomy: all its life it remains part of the mother. Two elements are important for the child's equilibrium: good relations with father and mother, and a satisfactory role for the father in society, i.e. by means of his professional life. The father must be an example, but he can no longer be an example in the same way as before: he works less and less under the eyes of his children, and the children work less and less in the same way as their parents. If the father can no longer teach his trade or craft to his son, he can at any rate give him the foundations of good behaviour, no matter what work the child may take up.

Following in father's footsteps does not necessarily consist in doing the same thing as one's father, but in doing it with the same degree of seriousness. The son may no longer see his father work, but leisure-time allows him to share in some of his activities. The quality of the father's presence is as important as the presence itself. Some fathers, who are at home a great deal, are away from it in their minds, while others, who are rarely there, have a very strong presence. The quality of the father's presence during leisure time is closely bound up with the satisfaction which he shows in his relationship with his wife and in his professional activity. The frustrations felt by the father at work inevitably rebound on his family life.

Now work in modern society is often frustrating; it must not be forgotten that fathers also suffer from being unable to demonstrate their personal abilities in their work, and in so doing find a way to fulfil their need for expression. They do not leave their personal mark on their work; in other words, nothing in what they do, in their papers or in their professional behaviour, reveals the individual who has done the work. This situation, together with the daily routine which repetition makes boring, supports a constant feeling of deception. The father is imprisoned in work which makes him suffer and which is incapable of satisfying his needs for creation and expression. To alleviate this situation he needs to have convictions. These convictions can be political, religious or philosophical. Unfortunately, modern society does very little to encourage people to have convictions. This is an important fact, because they are necessary for education and identification.

In an article on Willy Brandt, François Schlosser tells the following story:

> His grandfather was on strike and the owners of the Draeger factory decided on a lock out. Willy stared, round-eyed, in the window of a baker's shop; a passer-by, a director of the factory, offered him two large loaves of bread. Willy Brandt took them and rushed home, where for several days they had been utterly starving. All out of breath, he told his story. His grandfather, out on strike, was outraged; he got up and said to him: 'We don't want alms or presents. We want our rights.' Young Willy, deeply ashamed (he should have known that), took back to the baker's the two loaves which no one had wanted to touch. The grandfather had his convictions.

If so many young people today reject society totally and anarchically, is this not to compensate for the attitudes of their fathers? Are they not perhaps expressing the repressed feelings of their fathers? The rebellion against fathers would in that case be a rebellion against a belittled father who no longer did his job as a grown-up man. Why should young people be less rebellious? Should not the fathers be more so? Psychologists and sociologists have shown the importance of the father displaying his aggression in the presence of his children. If the father is never aggressive the child never feels protected. One of the important factors in neuroses is the contrast which is proposed as a norm and the reality which is experienced.

I have often had occasion to note that many fathers have abandoned all authority. When a child is brought for a psychological consultation it is usually accompanied by its mother, more rarely by both parents, and only exceptionally by the father alone.

A boy of sixteen was brought to me by his mother because of difficulties at school. He was taking his fifth year exams again without having any chance of passing the sixth year ones. According to what his mother said, he did not work because he was lazy. He had been a good pupil until he got to the fourth year. After the age of fourteen he did not seem interested in anything. I sent his mother out so that I could talk with the boy by himself. The so-called 'lazy' boy had no difficulty in explaining his attitude.

'It's true. I'm not interested in anything. But I think that the atmosphere at home is very much responsible for my boredom: my father comes home late, completely worn out. He is sales director at his office. When he talks, it's to complain about his work. He keeps saying that he's going to resign; he's had enough of being squeezed between his boss and the customers. My mother is always on my back. She keeps saying, "Work, work; if you go on like this, you'll never get a diploma." When I see my father, I wonder what the point of diplomas is. I was very interested in history. This year they've done away with all the books that I liked. I have to do maths and get into the sixth year scientific stream. That doesn't interest me. I don't want to be an engineer.'

'What do you want to do?'
'History.'
'What kind of job do you want?'
'I don't know.'
'Have you asked your father's advice?'
'He hasn't time. One day he said that if I did not do mathematics there was no point in my passing the school-leaving examination.'
'What are your hobbies?'
'None. The family's one obsession was for me to pass the leaving examination in the scientific stream.'
'What do you do on Sunday?'
'They have the television on.'
'And in the holidays?'
'We go to see my grandparents in the valley of the Lot.'
'Do you belong to a group or a young people's association?'
'My mother thinks it's a waste of time.'

I gave the boy tests to establish his IQ and his skills. The tests revealed an excellent intelligence with a leaning towards literature. The psychological examination confirmed an important opposition to his mother and the total absence of a father image. It was February. I asked for this 'intelligent lazybones' to go to a boarding school in the mountains which I knew well. In this establishment the teachers and pupils live very much together and half the day is devoted to cultural activities and sports. With the support of the admissions tutor, I managed to enter him in the literary stream. The father raised no objections whatsoever.

The boy has been there five years. He's now working for a degree in history and is preparing to go to the École Supérieure du Tourisme.

In our society in process of evolution, renunciation and oppression are not the only possible modes of education. The expression of aggressiveness and exchange are indispensable to the psychological development and the growth of individuals.

An open dialogue is necessary. I know many Christian parents who refuse to discuss with their adolescent children problems like the celibacy of priests, homosexuality, abortion, the pill, and so on. Some do not even have television, to avoid as far as possible the intrusion of dangerous information into family life. They reject all kinds of conversation apart from those which fall into the category of village pump gossip. Some consult doctors or psychologists over educational difficulties. Unfortunately, most often they come too late, when they have been completely overtaken by the aggressiveness of their children.

Psychological and sociological enquiries have shown that whereas, up to puberty, the father needs to show a degree of authority, thereafter relationship must be progressively more egalitarian. In this way the father acknowledges that his children have reached adulthood.

This recognition is the opposite of a paternalist and patriarchal attitude. Paternalism is characterized by the fact that the boss or the father are the only ones who have authority in matters of creation or management. In the patriarchal structure, the predominance of the father is accepted by all the members of the tribe. Now, authority is no longer a right: the one who holds it has to be recognized, accepted and identifiable.

For a long time the Jewish family retained a patriarchal structure: the oldest, father or grandfather, was the uncontested head of the family. I do not know what the current situation in Israel is. In France this structure has a tendency to disappear. The ancestor is respected, but his opinions no longer carry the same weight. Adolescents, like all their generation, claim their independence much earlier and do not allow others to decide their future or their marriage.

Information, dialogue and identification are the basic rules of modern education. Young people do not reject authority, but they do reject both authoritarianism and demagogy. They need to respect and admire those who have the responsibility for educating them.

I have often noted that a number of young priests, school chaplains, were themselves in contention with the paternal image and paternal authority. Unconsciously, they have a tendency to demagogy and to confuse systematic contention and education. Not least among the church's errors was its belief that it could have a role in the education of young people without going through the family circle, although it is true that education takes place more by osmosis and by symbiosis with the current cultural milieu than in a magisterial fashion. The teaching of the catechism has been given renewed life and vigour, but the question is to know whether this modernization has been effective. In the course of one of their meetings, school chaplains were asked about this question. They were aware that the young people whom they themselves had taken through the catechism according to the new norms, when they were children, were not more markedly Christians at the age of twenty than those generations which had been brought up on the old national catechism: they continued to have distorted views of God. 'The good news' can only interest those who have already had experience of the human condition. St Paul, like Jesus, spoke both to young people and to adults. The only time that a child listened to one of St Paul's homilies, the book of Acts tells us, he went to sleep and fell out of the window.

At present, Catholic Action movements (Young Catholic Farmers, Young Catholic Workers, Young Catholic Students) are in a state of crisis. They replaced the individualist morality of the last century with the social morality of the present century. The Young Catholic Farmers played an important role in the birth of a dynamic trade union movement. I think that the present crisis is due to two important facts: the young people cannot escape from the moralizing reductionism of Christianity, and their development has been blocked by the paternalism of the hierarchy.

The clerical hierarchy is still, in fact, paternalistic. The bishops attempt above all to reassure their people, telling them that all is well with the clergy. In his book *Questions to My Church*, Jean-Claude Barrault explains why he has been refused laicization.

The bishops rebuked him for telling the truth and not dissembling. That is what made Rome determined to refuse him laicization and to apply illegitimate blackmail: if you keep quiet, you will get your dispensation! If he had kept his secret, respected the appearances, he would have been given his dispensation. To justify this attitude, those responsible often quote a phrase taken out of context in the gospels: one must not cause the little ones to stumble. But like the curse against those who cause offence, these words are understood in a contrary sense to that in which they were intended. Jesus was not afraid of scandalizing the petty folk among his people with their prejudices, and the people of note with their hypocrisy. When he says that the weak must not be made to stumble, he is saying precisely the opposite of what the hierarchy wants to make him say. He tells the strong not to betray the confidence that the weak put in them. Is it not betraying the confidence of the grass-roots to deceive them, to lie to them, to throw dust in their eyes? Is that not to consider them irresponsible? In reality, an apparent refusal to scandalize the weak conceals a reactionary mentality and scorn for the people. Instead of reassuring and soothing words from bishops, one would prefer to hear the head of the church addressing Christians in these terms: 'Yes, it's true, there is a serious crisis. Many priests no longer accept the status people would like them to have. Let us look to see why, and try to find a way of remedying the situation.'

The Christian communities of the first centuries put this adage into practice: *vox populi, vox dei*, that is to say, the voice of the people is the voice of God. They did not establish this distinction between a teaching church skilled in interpreting the word of God and a taught church reduced to a passive attitude. After Pentecost, the first Christians were aware that they were living in a time of the Spirit and of liberty: prophets were legion. Alongside the legitimate authority of the bishops, coming from Christ and the apostles, there was the wild authority of the prophets, coming from the Spirit and the people. As Jean-Claude Barrault recalls, the Franciscan movement was the most typical of these evangelical movements which stirred up Christianity. Francis of Assisi, a nobleman's son, who used to run after girls, a poet who played the guitar, on hearing the gospel unleashed a prophetic movement which was one of the purest in the history of Christianity. The Friars Minor, God's fools, went naked in public places to provoke the middle-class. They spoke in churches to denounce the exploitation of man and injustice. These movements were the connecting tissue of the church. Now, the Christian institution seems to have lost its fundamental vitality. The more the basic cells become bloodless, the more the staff headquarters become overcrowded and bureaucratic. What will be the source of the Christian renewal which all Christians long for without actually saying so?

Secularization and sacralization. Is God dead?

Intoxicated with their technological triumphs, people ask about the need for God. Some have even gone so far as to prophesy his death. However, the metaphysical anxiety is always there, tormenting the spirits, torturing the hearts, creating a richer and more real call to the divine than perhaps in any other century. Beyond question, the problem is that God is no longer where people today are looking for him. We are witnessing a real process of secularization: man will no longer accept a certain image of God, and wants to take charge of the world in which he lives. This phenomenon is due to an upheaval in the relationships between man and nature: the primitive lived in a nature which dominated him, and he had to pander to it to obtain its benefits, to tame it by magic. God was regarded as the one responsible for all the natural phenomena: rain and fine weather, heat and cold. Only a merciful God who promised eternal life could make tolerable for mankind a nature which was more hostile than nurturing, a poor world in which technology had not succeeded in multiplying its riches. Earth was a 'vale of tears', and at Christmas the prayer was for the divine Messiah to come to 'save our unfortunate days.'

Science has analysed the natural phenomena and has proved that they obey laws, that they follow certain patterns, and in so doing it has done away with the quasi-permanent intervention of God. Technology has multiplied our riches. The earth is no longer a vale of tears, but a dwelling place which we are steadily building up in order to live in it. Man is learning to rely on himself. The American theologian Harvey Cox, author of *The Secular City*, affirmed, 'The world has become our business and our responsibility'. Farmers are now more interested in fertilizers than in rogations, those prayers they used to ask God to multiply the fruits of the earth. Those who earn salaries have more confidence in social security than in providence. Man is involved in the formidable adventure of the material transformation of the world. Henceforward his key words are no longer prayers, meditations, contemplation, but strategy and projects. Nature has been desacralized.

However, we must not confuse secularization and de-Christianization. It does not imply a generalized atheism: certainly it creates a framework in which atheism spreads more easily than faith and becomes the more normal attitude, which is more in keeping with the new state of the world. The fact that the world has become 'secular' does not constitute a defeat for Christianity: it is easy for

Christian theologians to show that the desacralization of nature and culture are in line with the gospel. The God whom Christianity proclaims is a God who has given over the world to man. Mgr François Marty, Archbishop of Paris, stressed this very strongly at a meeting of the Catholic Secretariat for Non-Believers at Vienna in September 1968: 'A good theology of creation will not be surprised at desacralization, given that the relationship between creature and creator is not sacred in the precise sense of the term. The more man constructs the world, the more God is creator. Secularization is not de-Christianization.' This development suggested to certain people that for modern man, God is dead. But God is not dead. What has disappeared is just God the magician, God the idol. Christians ought to rejoice at this, since the first communities made their appearance in ancient society as those who rejected idols and the gods of magic.

Modern man also rejects the image of God the policeman, who watches over every action in our life, and towards whom the only possible modes of relationship are guilt and anxiety: for a long time the church has been one of the chief structures of order and the transmission of culture. Society has organized itself, and the clergy can no longer hope to be the sole regulators of inter-personal relationships. Technology and culture have developed outside the church. The role of the church has been purified. In this way it is rediscovering its first vocation: to proclaim to modern man, with all his crises, the good news. The crises are evident: literary and artistic works regularly conclude that everything is absurd, and the rebellions of students move from one continent to another, bearing witness to an agonizing quest into the meaning of existence. Whereas man has had extraordinary success in his struggle to achieve mastery over nature, the same triumph has not been achieved in his efforts to organize social life rationally. This social life is always made up of conflicts, inequalities which make us blind, and relationships based on force. Science and technology have not destroyed mankind's irrational need. This need explains the proliferation of seers and astrologers, the development of strange sects, the new successes of Buddhism, the hippie phenomenon, the vogue of drugs, the multiplication of satirical shows. The hero of Pasolini's film *Theorem* expresses fear of loneliness and the absence of God as he runs naked in a desert of ashes, and his final, almost inhuman cry is not thrown back by any echo. The movement towards desacralization in nature is accompanied by a quest for a new sanctity.

Modern man has come to experience a new ill in his life. He is not master of himself as he is master of the universe. He sees that growing rationality is matched by growing absurdity. He is afraid that he is living out a senseless adventure. In Camus' words from *The Outsider*, 'And there is my old anxiety, there, at the pit of my stomach, like an unhealed wound which is irritated by every movement. I know its name. It is fear of eternal solitude. Fear that there is no reply.' Today we can note many signs of a real quest for God. In American universities, eighty per cent of the students have expressed the need for a spirituality and a religious faith. In French parishes, the priests who organize conferences on social problems have noted that they attract fewer people than those on faith. A few years ago, an issue of the American magazine *Time* bore the title '*Is God dead?*' shortly afterwards, it put the opposite question on the cover: '*Is God in the process of reviving?*' However, young people no longer accept a moralizing God.

Thus many images of God have been swallowed up or are on the point of being swallowed up: the God charged with coming to the help of people in difficulty has been increasingly supplanted by science. God who by way of recompense dispenses his benefits in heaven, after our vale of earthly tears, has also gone: modern man wants to have the right to succeed in this life.

Young people are looking for a God who will make sense of their life and allow them to flourish and be happy on this earth, a God who favours love, communication, fellowship between people. He is more effective than drugs. This God is a success at the theatre box office: Jesus is a super-star in a rock opera and *Godspell* is full of pop music hits on his name. I know numerous priests or even bishops who go to refresher courses at the theatre!

A few months ago, I saw again a student of twenty-seven, who had left to study sociology and psychology in the United States. He had come to consult me earlier for a depressive state which made it impossible for him to pursue his studies. Family atmosphere seemed to me to be the determining factor in his situation, and I had advised him to escape from the Catholic, neurotic and rigid world in which he lived. What he told me about the development of the Jesus movement particularly interested me.

Hundreds of thousands of young people are modelling themselves on the first Christians. Furthermore, it is striking to note how the United States resembles imperial Rome in the first century, by its enormous size which obliterates and represses the individual, its spiritual void, its overwhelming urbanism and its ponderous administrative uniformity. In this dehumanized world, Jesus has found a new clientèle: the Jesus freaks have replaced the left-wing drug addicts. They recruit all those who have followed through the sexual revolution to the end, or have made an attempt at purely political revolution: the drug addicts, the delinquents.

'Have you been to these prophetic assemblies about which people talk so much?'

'Yes, it's very impressive. There's usually a rock group at the meetings: trumpets, electric guitars, saxophones, electric piano, electric organ. These people play with their heart, with their guts. For them, to play rock songs is to pray and speak directly with Jesus. The walls and the ceilings shake. The whole gathering begins to shout and clap their hands to the rhythm of the music, singing songs and swaying to and fro. It's difficult to resist such an atmosphere. Then they go on to much gentler songs, with a slow rhythm: "Jesus is good, he loves us, he will come to save us." '

'Who directs this kind of meeting?'

'A brother who stands at the microphone and shouts, "I believe in one God, I renounce Satan for ever, I recognize that Jesus is the only saviour", and everyone repeats this act of faith phrase by phrase. Then the brother directing the meeting asks, "Are you saved?", and the whole gathering rises to its feet and shouts, "Yes, Alleluia", while the orchestra plays full force.'

'Who has formed this kind of community?'

'The one I've told you about was created by an average American group who were disgusted at everything, at society as it is, money, the struggle to live.'

'Have you seen strange phenomena like speaking in tongues, about which people have already told me?'

'No, but it seems that in some of these prayer meetings people get up and improvise speeches in languages which they themselves don't know. Linguists who have been given recordings of them are said to have identified one or other almost unknown dialect.'

'Do you believe it?'

'Such phenomena are described in St Paul's letters. They are said to have persisted even down to the second or third century.'

'Have the prayer meetings made much impression on you?'

I remained something of a spectator. I didn't succeed in belonging to that kind of gut religion, with its collective hysteria. I've been very much influenced by what is apparently a contradictory culture.'

'Contradictory?'

'Yes, by Teilhard de Chardin, Reich and Freud.'

'Really? What attracted you in the ideas of Teilhard?'

'This idea that the terrestrial globe is composed of a spherical mass of brute matter, wrapped in a thin covering like the skin of a fruit. This thin covering is formed by the whole of animal, vegetable and mineral life: he calls it the biosphere. This covering secretes another which is superimposed upon it, formed by all human thoughts which cross and recross like the threads of a fabric: the intellectual potential, the thought of humanity form this covering which grows greater every day. Progressively, matter is being transformed into thought, and our era will become less and less physical. At the end of a certain number of thousands or millions of years of evolution, there will be nothing round the earth but the noosphere, that is, this second layer of which Teilhard de Chardin speaks. It is at that moment that we shall encounter Jesus Christ. This conception of Teilhard is very interesting: all these infinitely small elements of which the universe is composed, atoms, cells, molecules, is destined finally, through being organized more and more to form a single thing. Teilhard calls this movement of the association and concentration of the thought of humanity "socialization". These ideas have certainly played an important role in the phenomenon of secularization and the desacralization of the church: Teilhard explains Jesus in the movement of biology, whereas Proudhon, for example, only explained him in a historical movement.'

'But you've also mentioned Reich. It's difficult to reconcile these two ways of thinking.'

'Yes, that's true. The only point they have in common is to try to liberate man from his anxiety and his difficulties in living and understanding the purpose of his life on earth. Reich defined Western civilization as being the reign of the patriarchal family. Before that, men lived in a primitive form of communism which was matriarchal. Sexuality was free, because when a woman had a child, no matter who the father was, this child was legitimate, and there was no problem in integrating it into the tribe. Everything began to deteriorate when certain people wanted to take land for themselves. The patriarchy developed to make it possible to keep it in the family after death and for the property to grow, and it brought with it marriage, the family and the notion of inheritance. Henceforward, sex no longer simply served the healthy and liberating joy of orgasm, but only the making of heirs. The sexuality of adolescents and the sexual liberty of adults had to be repressed. Orgasm was thought to be bad, and an ascetic morality developed.'

'Did this evolution take place well before the birth of Christianity?'

'Yes, Christianity reinforced it. The church has kept close to the patriarchal system, which was a repressive system, facilitating the maintenance of order and the transmission of established values. Furthermore, it is striking to note that all the apostles were men. Now the Holy Father always talks of his "very dear children".'

'Let's get back to Reich's ideas.'

'On some points, these ideas meet up with those of Freud: sex, man's innermost core, cannot be destroyed. Also, as is unexpectedly and brutally evident, this confirms puritan and clerical morality in the idea that man is bestial and diabolic. The greater part of the energy which should have been used in sexuality is diverted: perhaps outwardly, as sadism or the aggressiveness of war; or perhaps inwardly, in which case it is masochism and neurosis. Man surrounds himself with an armour of inhibitions which make a screen between his desires and the world. It seems that patriarchy made possible material development, but blocked the psychological, emotional and sexual development of mankind.'

'It is striking to note that May 1968 put the ideas of Reich into effect, although they were not very well known in the student world.'

'Yes, sexual revolution and community life. This development shows the gradual dissolution of the patriarchate and its entourage of inhibitors, prohibitions and taboos.'

'Do you think that Christianity is in danger, given the perspective of such a revolution?'

'Certainly, in its present form. It is an institution of a patriarchal type, based on a neurotic education, making use essentially of repression and suppression. However, Christ's first message remains more true than ever: "Love one another, as I have loved you." It remains the most powerful catalyst for future grass-roots communities, about which people have talked so much.'

It is interesting to note that this young man who was working at a thesis on 'The Patriarchal Society' is living in a community with students of his own age. There are eight of them: four women and four men. However, they have not put the sexual revolution into practice. The structure of couples has been maintained. I asked him why. He replied, 'We have not developed so far as to transgress all the traditional structures.'

The role of psychology and psychoanalysis

What is the place of psychoanalysis in this development of civilization? To understand the historical scope of Freud's work it is important to recall the conception of neurotic disturbance, as it existed in the second half of the nineteenth century.

For anatomical and clinical thought, the real foundation of a neurotic problem was a localized anatomical change in the nervous system. At that time hysteria was regarded as a hypnoid state of certain zones of the cerebral cortex. This state was capable of remission.

Physiological and pathological thought tried to interpret hysterical phenomena as deviations in the physical and kinetic process of the organism. Some researchers tried to reduce hysteria to a chemical formula. Others tried to make a clinical exploration of respiratory neuroses, with the aid of pneumographic exploration. Finally, research into the aetiology of neurotic disturbances explained them in terms of external traumas which in each instance seemed to determine them.

The work of Freud completely transformed the conception of neurosis, bringing into it dialogue with the patient and careful listening. The access to the patient is no longer simply visual and tactile. Listening and dialogue make it possible to reconstitute his or her psychological, emotional and social history. An interpretative attitude on the part of the doctor goes with this. Finally, the word ceases to be a pure instrument of research: it becomes a therapeutic agent.

Schematically, we could reduce Freud's contribution to four important points: the notion of libido, i.e., taking into consideration for diagnosis and treatment the instinctual elements of human life; the discovery of the existence of different levels of psychological awareness and the exact significance of their respective contents and the importance of these in the life of man; a decisive contribution to the exact knowledge of the influence exercised by the life of the spirit on the movements of the body; and reciprocally, the preoccupation with making intelligible in the history of the patient the event which is the patient's illness. Here the patient has become a person and not just a collection of physiological and physico-chemical mechanisms.

On some points the ideas of Freud come close to primitive Christian speculation. This speculation made a neat distinction between illness and actual sin, but it was able to perceive the possible secondary role of sin in the disturbance of the mind and the guilt which encouraged illness. Inversely, it showed the action of the physical illness on moral life, the significance of the fact that this illness is suffered by a person who gives meaning to it. In primitive

Christianity this idea of the relationship between moral life and physical life determined a double and complementary practice: concern for the emotions among spiritual directors, and watchful attention by doctors to reactions determined by the physical life which were capable of disturbing the moral life. As evidence for this, let me mention a letter from St Basil to his physician Eustathius, and the spiritual rule in the hospital of Caesarea which was the work of St Basil, towards 370. Gregory tells us that sickness was patiently borne in this hospital. Compassion was practised every day in the face of the suffering which came from outside. We are a long way from the attitude of pagans who, when there was an outbreak of plague in the third century, ran away from the sick, even their relatives, threw those who were dying into the street, and left the dead unburied.

Freud's thought parts company completely from primitive Christianity in connection with man's psychological development. He criticizes Christian doctrine for depreciating earthly life and having built up the structure of civilization on the principle of the renunciation of instinctive drives and their repressions. He writes: 'This cultural renunciation directs the wide domain of social relationships between human beings, and we know that this is the cause of the hostility against which all civilizations have to suffer.'

In his book *Civilization and its Discontents*, Freud explains that the greatest obstacle encountered by civilization is the constitutional aggression of human beings against others.

The collective superego promulgates moral laws which do not take account of the fact that the ego does not enjoy an unlimited authority over its id: even in the person who claims to be normal, the domination of the id by the ego cannot go beyond certain limits.

Freud thinks that the commandment 'Love your neighbour as yourself' does not take account of man's natural aggression, and represents the type of the anti-psychological conduct of the collective superego. It allows only one satisfaction, 'the narcissitic satisfaction of being able to think ourselves better than others'.

Freud also criticizes the fact that religions rely on the promise of a better world in the beyond. He writes: 'If virtue is not to be compensated in this world, I am convinced that ethics will be a voice in the wilderness.' Freud thinks that the Christian message is a factor of neurosis and anxiety because it requires of man an attitude which is not natural to him. It is true that for neurotics, discontented with themselves, the aggression which they have towards others is commensurate with the aggression that they show towards themselves, and the maxim 'Love your neighbour as yourself' does not make any sense to them. Freud would prefer this 'sublime commandment' to be formulated in a different way: 'Love your neighbour as he loves you himself.'

One of the important aims of psycho-analysis is to allow the neurotic to know himself better and therefore to accept himself better. From this perspective, Freud contradicts himself: it is impossible to accept others if we cannot accept ourselves.

In his book *The Murder of Christ*, William Reich expresses the idea that man's psychological difficulties are due to the suppression of all autonomy, from birth onwards. The newly-born is immediately subject to aggressions and prohibitions which provide him or her with an outer shell. That is why 'the character structure of man cannot be fundamentally changed, any more than a tree, having pushed through, can be shifted'. Reich thinks that we must direct all our attention to 'the newly-born in the world', to the small children born without this outer shell, which are still completely adaptable.

The aim of all psychotherapy is to give people this mobility. An education based on love and respect for the child will allow it to accept itself immediately as a subject capable of living without the need of a more or less rickety scaffolding.

Carl Rogers has described this development in *On Becoming a Person*:

> Each person must discover progressively that he can trust his own feelings and reactions, that his basic instincts are neither destructive nor calamitous, and that he does not need to be protected. He can confront life with an authentic face. In thus learning that he can have confidence in everything that is unique in him, he becomes more capable of having trust in others and accepting the feelings and unique values which exist in others.

Unfortunately, a number of individuals who are neurotic as a result of their education, while having a perfect understanding of the reasons for their behaviour, are incapable of really modifying it. 'Chase away the natural, and it will return at the gallop.' It is more accurate to say, 'Chase away inhibition and it will return at the gallop.' All education makes a profound impression on the brains of children and adolescents, and this impression is not only psychological: it is also biological. This is proved by current research into cerebral biochemistry and the peptide supports for the memory and behaviour. These results are based for the most part on the work of Professor Ungar in his laboratory in Houston, Texas. His experiments go through three stages. In a first stage he puts given animals through a course of training; in a second stage he prepares an extract from their brain; in a third stage he administers this extract to acceptor animals and watches for possible transmission of what has been learned.

The first experiments of this kind were made in 1962 with flatworms, which are worms with a very elementary structure. M. C. Connel gave these flatworms very simple training: they had to choose the right branch of a T-shaped labyrinth. Once the animals had been trained, he chopped them into little pieces and gave them as food to other flatworms. These other flatworms who had eaten their like learned more quickly.

The first experiments with superior animals were made in 1965. In 1968, Professor Ungar began experiments to make rats avoid the dark. These were particularly interesting, because it was the reversal of an innate natural tendency. Several thousand rats were trained to avoid the dark, which was made intolerable for them. Out of these millions of brains one substance, scotophobine, was isolated, which is a peptide formed by about fifteen amino-acids. This substance was injected into other animals, rats, mice, goldfish, in doses of about a millionth of a gramme. It made them avoid the dark for several days.

Recently, Professor Ungar has isolated a second peptide from the brain of rats conditioned by a sonic stimulus. When they hear a sudden sound, all the animals quiver; when the stimulus is repeated, the quivering disappears. Rats have been subjected to this sound every five seconds for ten to twelve days. The extract from the brain of these conditioned animals injected into other animals makes them indifferent to sonic signals. So training for several days or weeks is enough to change momentarily the innate behaviour of an animal or its reactions to a given stimulus. This change makes an impression on the brain, leading by chemical modifications to the formation of new substances which, injected into other animals, modify their behaviour. A neurotic education impressed on the brain over two years must produce profound biological modifications in those who have been given it. This new conception of a brain made up of millions of nerve cells between which tens of millions of connections and biochemical reactions are established during childhood and adolescence – the material trace of experiences, everyday discoveries and events undergone – explains the difficulties which people have in 'becoming', and in breaking out of their shells when education has made them infantile. How many men and women spend their whole lives fighting against their cerebral impressions and the indestructible connections in their brains? They ceaselessly relive stereotyped situations which make them feel anxious and guilty. How many men and women are incapable of having a normal sexual life because they are stamped with the fear of sexual sin? Things get more serious still when, with advancing age, people are less and less capable of learning and creating, because it becomes increasingly difficult to establish new connections. They can only continue in the same way. For Professor Lhermitte, the complaint one generation makes about another is not just a psychological phenomenon, but also a biological one. With age, the brain loses its plasticity and cannot adapt to new situations and ideas. In *The Murder of Christ*, William Reich asks why all dogmas about life-styles have gone bankrupt:

> The reply we must give this question is not the business of humanity fixed in immobility . . .We must distract the attention of suffering humanity from irrational precepts towards the new-born child, the eternal child of the future. Our task must consist in safeguarding his potentialities so that they can develop.

At his birth (perhaps even from his conception), the child is a blank page on which we have the power to write: love, self-confidence, respect for self and others, responsibility, liberty, learning, pleasure and renunciation, will establish much more creative connections than those induced by ideas of sin, guilt, prohibition and taboo which fix a human being in what Reich calls 'the emotional plague'.

Society in general and the Catholic church in particular are only what people make them. We must make a profound change in our conceptions if we wish by means of a preventive education to struggle effectively against collective neuroses. Modern research into heredity shows us that nature itself gives us the example of a dynamic evolution towards an increasingly perfect adaptation. Thus an organic force drives us to a perpetual progress: there is no incompatibility between a spirituality in which the essence of being finds its justification, its explanation, and its destiny, and a psycho-sociological evolution where the future and the changing model of the world is structured in influences, convergences and confrontations.

6

The Institutional Neurosis of the Church

A hypertrophied superego and an obliterated ego

Civilization is evolving, the Roman Catholic church is in a state of crisis. Why? What response is it making to the problems posed by changes in a society in the process of growth? In any business, if a third of the younger staff left, the directors would want to know why. Twenty thousand priests have left the ministry in the space of a few years, amounting to thirty per cent of priests under forty. Since the Council, the church has devoted all its strength to the reform of its institutions. Was it necessary, for all that, to double the staff of the Roman Curia on the pretext of making it international? Was it necessary to multiply committees, sub-committees, liason committees and so on? A number of priests and bishops spend most of their time making the institution work. With a hypertrophied superego, rigid and anxious, and an obliterated ego, trying to survive in outmoded structures, the church, like all neurotics, is bad at communicating with itself and with the world around. Incapable of being creative, the institution, anxious and tense, is always on the defensive. It cannot adapt to a rapidly developing situation and always reacts with a certain time-lag. One could have wished, for example, that the social doctrine of the church had preceded the *Manifesto* of Karl Marx. Obsessed with its personal problems, the institution is turning in on itself. The church reminds one of those travellers who are always late, who have never stopped getting ready, jump on the train as it's going – and then discover they've caught the wrong one.

The superego of the church is hypertrophied. In the last century, the central government of the church identified itself with the monarchical model. Against all theology, the Catholic church had become an absolute monarchy in which only the sovereign had the right to speak. Bishops were no more than delegates of the Pope, governors of provinces. Numerous obsequious theologians exalted the role of the papacy, basing themselves on scriptural texts used wrongly. The First Vatican Council, in proclaiming papal infallibility, marked the climax of this development, which went against the gospel. In fact, the Vatican remains the last of the courts of Europe. Vatican II corrected this monarchical tendency. The Constitution on the Church recognizes the role of the people of God and stresses that of the bishops and the college which they form. It accepts the existence of national or continental churches. In fact, though, nothing has changed. Power has apparently been modernized, and the folk-lore has been shed. But the church is still just as centralized. The model is no longer the monarchical or the democratic state, but the great capitalist industrial society, with its public administration. The Roman Curia has twice as many officials as it did before the Council, that is to say, several thousand. It centralizes everything, and everything continues to go there and come from there. Certainly, it has been internationalized, because hundreds of non-Italian priests and prelates have been summoned there. But bishops continue to be nominated and to be closely controlled by it. My personal experience allows me to say that this control is particularly coercive. I produced a medical certificate for a prelate under my care, supporting his request for a reduction and rearrangement of his work. As is the custom, I produced this certificate without giving details of his illness, as these are a matter of professional secrecy. Some days later I received a telephone call from the nunciature ordering me to give a very detailed certificate.

'But, Monsignor, in no way can I violate professional secrecy.'

'We know what professional secrecy is.'

'I find your remark quite out of place.'

'I will send a car at five o'clock today. Prepare the certificate so that the chauffeur can take it. The diplomatic bag goes at 7 o'clock.'

'First I will ask what my patient thinks.'

'Let me reassure you, doctor, he will certainly agree.'

Some minutes later I spoke to my patient on the telephone and put the question to him. He told me that his only course was to obey.

The Pope is now the Chairman and Managing Director of a great multinational company. Not being able to deal with all its concerns by himself, he delegates his powers to curial prelates who, under the name of the Holy See, hold important responsibilities and, by being anonymous, escape criticism. As a sovereign state, the Vatican maintains diplomatic relations with all the governments of the world through the intermediary of a body of accredited diplomats, the corps of apostolic nuncios. These ecclesiastics are trained at a specialized school, the school of Vatican diplomacy. Papal ambassadors to national goverments, they are also charged with keeping a watch on local churches and suppressing their hankerings after autonomy. Often the local clergy calls the nunciature the denunciature. The nuncios play a decisive role in episcopal nominations. The chief officials of the curia and the Pope himself are chosen from among them.

When the Pope has something to say to a government, he prefers to use a discreet diplomatic approach. Thus his action remains secret. This diplomatic compromise explains why the Pope only denounced in a veiled and ambiguous way the torture used in Brazil by a government which claimed to be Christian. Well aware of the reality of Nazi concentration camps, Pius XII preferred to act in the secrecy of chancelleries. As François Mauriac said, 'It all meant that certain words which should have been spoken were not.' St Paul said that the church should speak in season and out of season, and did not have the right to negotiate.

The apostolic nuncios are themselves tightly controlled. Forty of them met in a Salesian villa at Frascati, in September 1973: their agenda was essentially the study of relationships between apostolic nuncios and conferences of bishops, and between the nuncios and the Curia. The Vatican diplomats have complained of particularly difficult relationships with the Curia and of being very often short-circuited by the bishops in Rome.

In France, the superego is also organized. Over the last few years we have seen the multiplication of administrative staff, directors and national centres. The most brilliant priests have been drawn into a kind of techno-structure, completely cut off from the grass roots. In Paris, for example, a diocese which is short on priests, one can count dozens of the most dynamic ones who are working in seven or eight different directions. As an example, let me take these comments by a priest of thirty-five whom I see regularly in hospital. He came to consult me some months ago for a depressive state of exhaustion, associated with sciatica which resisted all therapy.

'How long have you had these pains?'

'Two years.'

'What were you doing three years ago?'

'I was a parish priest working with youth groups.'

'And now?'

'I'm concerned with the training of priests, and retraining them at diocesan level. I have a degree in sociology and that's why I was given this job.'

'How long ago?'

'Two and a half years.'

'What does your job consist of?'

'Being present on committees and in information-gathering sessions. In addition I give courses in different seminaries.'

'Do you do a lot of travelling?'

'Endlessly. I travel between Paris, Nancy, Toulouse and Bordeaux.'

'You've become a commercial traveller?'

'If you like to put it that way.'

'Are you satisfied with this mode of living?'

'I have the impression that I'm wasting my time in tiring and useless journeys.'

'Has this been going on for long?'

'As long as I could bear it!'

'You couldn't refuse?'

'For what reason?'

'Because you couldn't take it physically and morally.'

'It's difficult to say. Those aren't valid arguments.'

'All right. I cannot continue to treat you in these circumstances. You must have a rest from work, and at the same time I shall demand, by whatever hierarchical course you may propose, to have you appointed to a fixed post. That is the only way of curing you.'

It took three months off work for the priest and a large number of certificates to obtain the change I required. This priest has now been appointed to Paris, where he has a national chaplaincy. His sciatica has disappeared. At our last interview he told me that for two years he had had the impression of being treated as an object.

The institutional church defends the patriarchal structure, while it is increasingly losing vitality at the grass roots. The rigid and hypertrophied superego, represented by Roman authority, does not take much account of the desires of the ego, formed by the mass of Christians. In the face of the rightful claims of this ego, the superego reacts with an apparent benevolence which conceals a profound rigidity. Roman authority often seems to lack good sense, let alone a critical spirit: it 'argues off the point' (this expression corresponds almost exactly to the etymological definition of the Greek word *paranoia*). In 1973 the church associated itself with the fifth centenary of the birth of Copernicus. Copernicus was born in Poland on 14 February 1473. In a letter to Cardinal Wyszynski, Paul VI praised this man of the church (Copernicus was a canon) who had been able to establish 'an admirable and fruitful link between faith and science'. But Paul VI forgot to say that it was not until 1822 that the church authorized the printing of books discussing the movement of the earth as a physical reality. Nicolas Copernicus was the first scientist to think in terms of an earth revolving around a fixed sun. The interpretation given by the church was incompatible with such an idea. For the church, man lived in a finite universe with the immobile earth at the centre. It had kept to the Aristotelian view of cosmology: 'The earth is a minuscule point at the centre of the universe, of which it is the kernel. For it, all the rest was made. That is where man lives, and the character of this region is very different from that of the celestial region situated above. The heavens are composed of an imperishable, incorruptible matter, alien to the universe, which is not marked by change and death as we know them.' This conception of the world corresponded to belief in a biblical God who put man at the centre of the universe in a place marked by change and death, but surrounded by a glorious sphere, the seat of divinity and immortality. In 1633 Galileo was forced to recant, when his scientific discoveries and observations continued the work of Copernicus, correcting it and developing it. The church took three hundred years to establish an 'admirable and fruitful link between faith and science'.

The coercive attitude of Roman authority and its tendency to 'argue off the point' have hardly changed. The condemnation of Teilhard de Chardin is just one indication of that. It was not until eighteen years after his death that the greater part of his writings, including notes and most intimate letters, were published. This posthumous publication so soon afterwards, of the least reflections of a man whose voice the authorities sought to quench, prohibiting not only all publication but also all communication outside strictly scientific questions, was a strange development. However, it seems that the Roman authorities have a great deal to learn from this great man of the church.

There are not many things in which I believe. But they are: first, and fundamentally, the value of the world; secondly, the need for our Christ, to give this world a consistency, a heart and a countenance. The only thing that I can be is a voice which repeats, in season and out of season, that the church will perish if it does not escape from the factitious world of verbal theologies, quantitative sacramentalism and devotions in which it enwraps itself, to reincarnate itself in real human aspirations. If Our Lord is as great as we believe, he will know how to guide my efforts in such a way that nothing breaks. I want no more than to live passionately in faith, a twofold faith in the world and in Christ.

What is the present situation? Is the institutional church evolving? Is its superego continuing to be hypertrophied, creating committees and sub-committees whenever a problem is raised? Is it really interested in its ego, in the conjunctive tissue on which its survival depends? For me, the advent of John XXIII was a source of hope. John XXIII loved people more than power. Thanks to him, the papacy at last seemed to accord with the gospel. He realized the unanimity of the world. He appeared as a universal father, without paternalistic pretensions, a possible ecumenical pastor, and he made the walls of mistrust crumble. The ego and the superego of the church began to communicate, but with great speed the neurotic institution reacted: the Roman authorities have now published a new document entitled *Mysterium Ecclesiae*. Once more, the rigid and authoritarian superego has obliterated the ego, suffused with love and brotherhood. This declaration was approved by Paul VI on 11 May 1973 and was signed on 24 June by Cardinal Seper and Monsignor Hamer. It was made public on 7 July. In fifteen pages it discusses four problems, and is aimed at protecting the Catholic church from four main errors: it is almost a contradiction, point by point, of the openings brought about by Vatican II. The declaration recalls that there is only one church. This church subsists in the Catholic church, governed by Peter's successors and the bishops who are in communion with him. It alone is rich with all the truth revealed by God, and all the means of grace. How about that for a declaration capable of favouring ecumenical developments? In a second chapter the declaration stresses the infallibility of the Pope. It recalls that the role of the Pope, successor of Peter and the other apostles, is to teach the faithful in an authentic way, i.e. by virtue of the authority of Christ. This *magisterium* of bishops and the Pope is not based on new revelations, but on the guidance of the Holy Spirit. It does not free them from the need to examine, by appropriate means, the treasure of divine revelation, in Holy Scripture and in living tradition. It is fortunate that the Pope and the bishops still have the right to reflect and to call for the help of the Holy Spirit.

The third point of the declaration recalls that all the dogmas, whatever they may be, must be equally believed to be of divine inspiration. The fourth point is by far the most retrograde. It is concerned with the priesthood. 'The ministers of the priesthood (this is the way in which the document describes bishops and priests on several occasions) receive a mark of Christ, a character which delegates them to their charge, furnishing them with an appropriate power, derived from the supreme power of Christ.' Thus, those faithful who celebrate the eucharist without having received priestly ordination, are performing an invalid act. In this passage of the declaration, the vocabulary is very classical: ministerial priesthood, hierarchy, power, character, and so on. Contemporary research is completely ignored.

John XXIII opened the window and Paul VI did not close it again. I hope that we are witnessing the renaissance of the church, which would thus prove to be the only institution capable of reforming itself. The Roman authorities, through the voice of the Congregation for the Doctrine of Faith, have rapidly taken things in hand. In fact the text they produced is partly directed against the Swiss theologian Hans Küng, whose books offer a very intelligent criticism of Roman authority. *Le Monde* published his reply to it. There he expressed the idea that this text was written in a pre-conciliar spirit and that it closes the doors opened by Vatican II. It blocks all further progress in the theology of ecclesiastical renewal and ecumenical agreements. Küng expressed the hope that the Congregation for the Doctrine of the Faith will develop, and that instead of being an organ of inquisition it will one day become an organ of evangelization. Küng was thereupon summoned to Rome and asked to explain himself. He agreed on condition that the process should be fair and equitable. For this to be so, he asked to have access to dossiers, to have the choice of a defence counsel and the possibility of appeal. All these conditions would be accepted in a civil trial. Unfortunately, they are not provided for by the Roman inquisition.

We fall back into the extremely pernicious scholastic distinction between a teaching church, only capable of interpreting the role of God, and a church which is taught, confined in passivity. Once again the Roman authorities behave like a paranoid personality which 'argues off the point' and does not accept being put in question. People always ask what Rome is defending by taking up categorical positions. I have always been struck by the fact that the papal documents propagate more of a morality and an anthropology than the gospel. The Popes hardly used their standing to proclaim 'the good news in season and out of season'.

The church forms part of what English-speaking people call 'the establishment'. In this way they underline the solidarity which exists between all the institutions of a certain age and which carry a certain weight, even when they claim to be opponents. The directors of the clerical apparatus come from the same world and have the same psychological reactions as those who direct nations. This compromise proved blinding at the time when Rome condemned the worker-priest experiment. However, unlike the politicians who control nations, the Catholic hierarchy is scarcely concerned with its majority. It is true that it has not subjected itself to the test of elections. It spends by far the greater part of its time setting up prohibitions and defences to block the concern to renew the ego, and forgets that it is among believers that questions about the meaning of the word of God and the language which can express it in intelligible terms for present-day man are born and develop. Faith proves to be less and less capable of being transmitted by words; it is enough to note the massive desertion of the younger generation, in particular those young people born in Christian families, to be persuaded of this. This fact is relatively new. In 1972–73, for the first time, there were no first-year seminarians in the Major Seminary of Issy-les-Moulineaux. The Roman authorities were utterly responsible for this state of affairs. The institutional neurosis is not an empty phrase: a neurotic patient cannot adapt; he is too preoccupied with the tensions which exist between his ego and his superego. In *Mysterius ecclesiae*, Rome is settling its account with a turbulent ego the drives of which cannot be contained for long.

According to an opinion poll published in *La Croix*, twenty-one per cent of French people go to mass regularly, whereas ninety-five per cent are baptized. Apparently the number of real faithful is declining, whereas that of the disciples of Jesus is constantly growing. The extraordinary success of the Jesus movement reported from the United States is a remarkable proof of this. Young people are in search of spirituality: more than ever, they are ready to hear the good news announced by Christ. Faced with this reality, the institutional church should no longer neglect essentials at the expense of details. It must realize that the majority of Christian institutions are completely out of touch, even when they have been created recently. The parishes are territorial areas, the product of a rural mediaeval world in which the village existed as a total human community. The cities were no more than federations of villages, which is clear from the structure of Venice, as explained by Le Corbusier: each village district was gathered around its church, its village hall, its market place and its well. The city gathered these districts around the Piazza San Marco, its basilica and the Doges' palace. In the urbanized and industrial world of today, villages have disappeared. In the country there is no longer true human community, and there are thousands of country clergy attached while still alive to the corpses of their parishes. Some react and leave their church, to discover the world around. I might quote the case of a country priest who for the first time last year paid a visit to the camp-site established in his parish. In this place of 'undress', as he humorously put it, he discovered a whole new throbbing world. A grass-roots community, formed of young people who since then have come every day to his morning mass (one of them, a veteran hippie, is preparing for the priesthood). A university teacher, a geologist, who told him the history of the part of the world in which he lived. A trade unionist with whom he discussed the LIP affair and worker participation. They are often in agreement.

'I would never had done that several years ago,' he told me with his nice smile. He is sixty. I've known him for a long time. This year I found him younger than ever, happy and enthusiastic. This traditional churchman is becoming more and more a communicator, a bond between men and God.

In the towns we have the realm of the masses, that 'lonely crowd' in which individuals get lost. Urban parishes often seem like service stations where an anonymous crowd comes to be consumers of the cult. Very often the priests are only officials, without any real relationship to people whom they barely know, apart from a small group of the faithful. The dimension of brotherhood no longer exists in these meetings, where people behave as if they were in cinemas with continuous performances. Without real community, the priests despair and grow stale, and the more demanding Christians become discouraged. Some time ago I treated the senior priest of a parish in the neighbourhood of Paris. He had come to see me for what one might call 'neurotic asthenia', that is, tiredness with a psychological origin. In the course of one of our first conversations he told me that he was losing his younger parishioners, who preferred to take part in the activities of the chaplaincy at the local school, where they found more communication and human warmth than in his almost historic monument.

'I sometimes wonder what I'm still doing in my church.'

'Perhaps you should leave. . . But are there only young people in your parish?'

'Yes, of course there are others, but the youth are the most dynamic element. I sometimes feel as if I'm looking after an old peoples' home.'

'Don't exaggerate. . . What is the average age of your parishioners?'

'Seven o'clock mass is attended by a majority of good sisters about whose age it is difficult to be certain. At 8 o'clock mass there are lots of old women and some retired men.'

'And on Sunday?'

'The mass for young people is less and less well attended.'

'I thought that there was no mass at the school chaplaincy on Sundays.'

'I believe that many of the young people who go to the activities of the chaplaincy during the week do not come to Sunday mass because it is compulsory and because it is the parish mass.'

'Perhaps they're bored.'

'That could be a reason. In my day, mass was not considered an entertainment.'

'Certainly, but there's quite a difference between an entertainment and being bored.'

'Young people have lost the sense of communal prayer and of the sacred.'

'The church has contributed to that. Mass should be a joyful and enriching gathering. Put yourself in the midst of the faithful at any Sunday mass, it doesn't matter which. Most of them are bored, yawning, thinking of something else. They sit down and get up like robots. One often feels it's a meeting of robots. The sermon is very often of doubtful interest. A simple commentary on the gospel could replace the sermon with benefit. As for the sacraments, they have too often been reduced to rites; that's why young people abandon them.'

'There, I think you're exaggerating.'

'Hardly. . . I would go even further. Some priests use the sacraments as a means of pressure on Christians about whom they are doubtful, i.e. whom they judge. They very often present the sacraments as a reward for good conduct. I ask whether Jesus would have had the right to sacraments.'

'Do you often treat people who don't believe in medicine?'

'More often than you might think. Some of them still believe in

doctors, which is something. But many of them don't believe in
anything, which explains why they resort to homeopathy, acupunc-
ture, yoga, a macrobiotic diet, all at the same time.'
'What do you tell them?'
'Nothing, I try to establish communication, a person-to-person
relationship with them.'
'Do they follow your advice?'
'It's impossible to give any statistics. In fact, that isn't the problem;
some of them never come back, others five years later. Some
"unbelievers" are converted.'
'Converted to what?'
'To the idea that they are not passive victims of incomprehensible
symptoms, but subjects who experience and favour their illness
without knowing it.'
'All the same, our jobs are very different; people have precise
reasons for coming to see you, they have headaches, stomach
aches . . .'
'Seventy per cent of the urban clientèle is made up of patients
suffering from what one might call functional illnesses; their troubles
are essentially due to their anxieties and the difficulties they find in
adapting. You are as capable as I am of relieving them and perhaps
even of curing them.'
'How?'
'By listening to people and avoiding being "directive". The
relationship between the priest and Christians is too often blocked
by kind, reassuring and inappropriate words.'
'Do you think that priests should have psychological training?'
'Yes, among other things.'
'We're a long way from that.'
'But that's the only solution. Like general practitioners, you will
disappear if people don't give you a psychological and perhaps even
psychoanalytical training.'
Since this conversation, my senior priest had been thinking. He
came back to see me some months later. He agreed to become
involved in group dynamics. He now comes regularly. At the end of
one of our last conversations, he explained that his relationship with
his parishioners had changed completely: his 'clientèle' had grown
substantially and he now had people coming on three afternoons a
week.
'What is the average age of your clientèle?' I asked him.
'It's going down: last week I had about a dozen young people
between eighteen and twenty-five years old.'

'What did they come to ask you?'

'Nothing, they came to talk.'

'Do they come to talk to the man, the priest or to a father image?'

'I don't know . . . they just come.'

A case of this kind might be entitled 'the abandoned priest'. In fact it would be better to talk about the under-educated or the under-informed priest. In this connection, I remember a conversation I had with a scout chaplain who came to consult me about intractable insomnia. He quickly came to the problem which preoccupied him most: his relationship with the young people under his charge.

'I no longer know how to react. I feel completely out of date, I might even say I'm not with it. Many young people are more competent than I, and I am incapable of replying to them and defending this or that position taken by the hierarchy of the church. The chief of the troop is at the School of Political Science, and I'm incapable of having a discussion with him. For example, he demonstrated that the problem of the atomic bomb was now solely a political one and that the position taken by certain bishops was ridiculous, because it was much too late. In 1945, such a campaign would have been of interest, but now it is quite out of place . . .He explained that France had to have the bomb to be able to enter the atomic club and share in discoveries which would enable us to renew our sources of energy. He affirmed that Willy Brandt was a Marxist and that he had a more or less secret desire to bring about the unification of Germany under the aegis of the Soviet Union. If France is not sufficiently strong, Europe will be dominated by the Soviet-German bloc. What do I say in reply? I've no political training.

I'm not much better informed about sexual education. One of the assistants is studying medicine. In the course of a meeting about the sexual knowledge of our young people he defended the need for pre-marital experience, with arguments which I found difficult to refute. He developed the idea of trial marriage, explaining it was the only way of eliminating certain sexual incompatibility which, if discovered after, might spoil couples' happiness. He even insisted on the necessity of a community life. I was incapable of responding to him. In the same meeting, which was made up of boys from sixteen to twenty, the problem of the virginity of girls was touched on. A student in psychology expressed the idea that this notion of virginity was simply cultural: in certain African ethnic groups, virginity was considered to bring evil, and defloration was effected before marriage by mechanical means. Among the Tibetans, it seems, a virgin is not desirable because if she is still a virgin it means that no one wanted her and therefore that she is useless. I feel incapable of playing my part. I am content to be an attentive and useless listener. The ideas presented to me put in question everything that I've learnt.

The psychology student who came to stimulate the meeting I've mentioned explained that in our civilization the idea of virginity has lost its originally positive sense as a value (purity, integrity, as identified with a strength sufficient to conquer wild animals) and has become a market value: just as meat must be fresh, a girl must be a virgin to find a purchaser. Several reasons would explain this conception: a psychological reason: because a women is an object to possess, one is more certain of really possessing an object when it does not yet belong to anyone; a social reason, to avoid the risk that hereditary patrimony will be passed on to bastards.'

'And why do these ideas prevent your sleeping?'

'The language and the culture of the young people in my charge are so different from mine that I no longer dare express myself. This evening, I had brought a little work reproducing in its entirety the speech given by the Pope to the Society of Our Lady on 4 May 1970. The title was "Sexuality, Marriage, Love".'

'Did you tell them about it?'

'No.'

'Why?'

'I was afraid of looking ridiculous.'

'I know the text, and it seems to me to have some interesting ideas.'

'Yes, but the form embarrasses me. I find it rather out of date, and also a bit too repressive. Look (he took the book out of his pocket), see what it says on page 9.'

The title of the chapter is 'Education in an Erotic Climate'. This is the actual text:

This teaching still retains all its value today and warns us against the temptations of a ravaging eroticism. This aberrant phenomenon should at least alert us to the distress of a materialist civilization which is taking bewildered soundings in this mysterious realm, like a last refuge of a sacred value. Can we protect it from getting bogged down in sensuality? Given the invasion cynically carried on by the consumer industries, can we at least throttle the evil effects of eroticism among the young? Without blockade or repression, we need to favour an education which helps the child and the adolescent to become progressively aware of the force of the drives which are awakening in them and integrate them into the construction of their personality, mastering the mounting forces in such as way as to realize a full emotional maturity, as well as sexual maturity, in that way preparing for a gift of the self in a love which will give it its true dimensions, in an exclusive and definitive manner.

'In this text the Pope is simply condemning eroticism and sensuality.'

'That is precisely what troubles me. Our young people are not really agreed about this kind of condemnation. They think that eroticism and sensuality are necessary to a couple's equilibrium. They condemn what they call "making policeman's love".'

'In antiquity there were matrons for domestic tasks and concubines for pleasure.'

'Young people now want their wives to be their mistresses as well.'

'That seems to be a sensible idea.'

'In your view, is there any incompatibility between sexuality, eroticism and Christian marriage?'

'No, Christians must be persuaded that they have the right to play.'

'Play, pleasure, are words I never heard at major seminary.'

'Times are changing. . .'

'Unfortunately, I'm not up with them. I find it difficult to talk about things of which I know nothing.'

'Yes, I think that's the real problem. Perhaps your insomnia is due to the fact that you brood too much on all these stories. That kind of meeting doesn't seem to be much help.'

'They excite me and overwhelm me at the same time. I wonder whether my place isn't in the Salvation Army?'

'That's not the same kind of work. You would have to learn to play the trumpet.'

'No, I would take round magazines and be in charge of the collecting tin.'

'Don't you think it would be wiser to complete your training?'

'Yes, but how?'

'I can put you under one of my friends who teaches at the University of Vincennes. He will introduce you to permanent training groups made up of students and workers. He also organizes seminars held over several days.'

That conversation was six months ago. I know from the colleague to whom I entrusted this priest that he goes very regularly to the groups he joined. I didn't see him again.

How many priests are anxious, simply because they feel incapable of fulfilling their role as educators, confronted with youth in possession of a great deal of information but without the common standards which they had. Their training in 'ghetto seminaries' explains the difficulty they find in responding, their anxiety and their guilt feelings: whether it is a matter of political, sexual or educational problems, generally speaking, the catechism which they learnt is quite insufficient. The young people no longer accept education on the basis of ready-made judgments, prohibitions and taboos. They want to understand, to know and to be responsible. Traditional neurotic education needs to be replaced with education in answering the question 'why'. If one believes in the gospel, I do not see why the hierarchy of the church should not accept this development.

Certain priests, on the other hand, develop of their own accord and adapt very well to a given situation, like the old priest from the Mission de France appointed to a country parish in the Nièvre. I and the Superior of Pontigny (to whom I was psychological consultant) had considerable hesitations about letting him be ordained priest. Fifteen years ago he was very anxious and ceaselessly complained of digestive troubles. Since then I have regularly kept track of him in my hospital consultations: in the first years his digestive troubles continued, and I saw him every two or three months. Then, little by little, I watched his behaviour change. He blossomed, put on weight, and his colitis gradually disappeared. After several years, during which he remained in complete isolation, he decided to move out from his church. He was there only on Thursday for catechism, Saturday afternoon for confessions and Sunday for mass. He spent the rest of his time making hay, hunting or fishing with his parishioners: in short, he lived with them and felt, as he told me, like a man among men. I saw him again several months later and asked him how his colitis was. He told me with a smile, 'It's completely disappeared since I became a whole man.'

The conjunctive tissue of the church is not just formed by priests: the laity make up its fabric. How do they behave?

There are the classic robots, law-abiding and well regulated . . . at least as long as they don't go off the rails. That is when the drama occurs. As evidence, let me mention the case of a senior official, very distinguished, very cultured, father of a large family, the perfect Christian, who discovered sexual pleasure and eroticism at the age of sixty-two. . . He left everything, wife and children, and happily lavished his fortune on his young mistress in so far as his coronaries and his cerebral arteries did not condemn him to the life of a total invalid.

I tried to treat this man, for whom I had the greatest sympathy. He returned home several times. He could never bear to be parted from his mistress for more than a few days. He acted like a real drug addict. After two years of this game, which made all treatment impossible, I asked him to rest at home for a month. I didn't see him again.

The great majority of middle-aged Christians keep their religious automatism by carefully avoiding putting it in question. To express their aggression, they fight for or against liturgical renewal. They are integralists or anti-integralists. The women teach the catechism without passion; the men are busy with St Vincent de Paul meetings. Sunday masses, the major festivals, and contributing to the collection serve as their fixed points. They wait for directives from the hierarchy before tolerating certain modifications to their routine religion.

Some, usually the younger ones, are involved in politics, under the direction of young priests who produce Marxist slogans. They have the impression of being in the front line, being against fine ceremonies, against the Latin mass and above all against the middle class. In short, what counts is being against everything that exists. Right-wing clericalism has been replaced by left-wing clericalism. Was Jesus right-wing or left? He was probably a free man, whose only words were words of universal love. Everyone claims him, and it is not one of his least qualities to be with all and for all.

The 'ego' of the church is very heterogeneous. It survives as best it can in this great shambles, trying to detect what remains of the message of the gospel. Fortunately, many signs bear witness to a true renewal: grass-roots communities, charismatic groups and above all lay participation in taking charge of numerous activities which were formerly reserved for priests. Ecumenism is making progress. Young Christians try to get together. They are aware that Roman authority is dominated by a doctrine, whereas Jesus was the servant of a liberation. There is discussion of the doctrines which are taught. Little by little, a new church is being built up at the grass roots, a new ego which is increasingly less prepared to be made infantile by a superego whose *ex cathedra* directives it no longer accepts. More than ever, we have entered a time of listening, sharing and real communication. But can one ask of an anxious Pope, a neurotic institution, a clergy which is trying to get back on balance, profound changes in an education which originates in a real collective neurosis? Paul Valéry made the relevant point: 'If the ego is hateful, to love one's neighbour as oneself becomes an atrocious irony.'

The Pope denounces the decline in morals[9]

'One ideal ceaselessly animates the church of God, and will continue to do so: to realize in itself, and to proclaim to the world around, the Christian message, the true Christian life as it emerges from the gospel and its authentic tradition. The demands of this ideal become more pressing in our post-conciliar age, given the numerous and often disordered phenomena which can be found even within the church over recent years. These phenomena have long been brewing in some coteries more open to the degrading currents of a secularized Christianity than to the living impulses which emerge from the depths of the faith. This ideal calls for a more urgent commitment, also taking into account the proximity of the Holy Year – and I would hope that this Holy Year would make the people of God feel serene in the awareness and the profession of their authentic vocation.

Now these courageous resolutions awaken in us the feeling and indeed the experience of the difficulties encountered today by an authentic Christian life. Christianity is not easy, especially in our age. At present there is a movement of thought and action, more headstrong than wise, which gives public opinion the formulas of a simple Christianity, voided of its profound demands, which is imperceptibly being assimilated to ideas current in the world. What I have just said about faith, I could also apply today in one sense to morality.

Is the Christian moral life easy today? No, dear brothers and sons, it is not easy. The observance of Christian morality constitutes one of the chief difficulties for the ethical and religious renewal that we could wish for. I am not saying that to frighten you and to rob you of any hope of success; but out of a sense of duty and in all sincerity, and to exhort you to courage in present circumstances. I tell you this first because at all times faith in Christ has required this realistic view of things and this courage. "It is not those who say to me, 'Lord, Lord,' who will enter the kingdom of heaven, but those who do the will of my Father who is in heaven" (Matt. 7.21; Rom. 2.13; James 1.25). "Go in by the narrow gate; narrow is the gate and hard is the road which leads to life" (Matt. 7.13f.). "If anyone would come after me, let him deny himself, take up his cross and follow me. He who seeks to save his life will lose it, and he who seeks to lose his life for my sake will save it" (Matt. 16.24f.). Those are the very words of Jesus. It is certain that the apostles and the first Christian generation saw in these words the demands for rigorous asceticism imposed by the new Christian moral law, as is evidenced, for example, by the Letter to Diognetus and the letter of St Ignatius of Antioch to the Romans.

Such an urgent exhortation to detach ourselves from outward and temporal possessions, this exaltation of the poverty of the spirit, the sequence of the Beatitudes which makes sweet fragrance arise from the bitterness of life and the heroic virtues of our existence here on earth, forgiveness for offences, the presentation of the left cheek to the one who strikes us on the right, purity of heart which goes even so far as to inhibit all dishonesty, all these demands form the fabric of the gospel which moves the human truth of good and evil from a legalistic and external morality to the intimacy of the heart (cf. Matt. 15.11). Now all that certainly makes it difficult to perfect Christian virtues. But we know that these renunciations are compensated for by love of God and love of the neighbour, a synthesis of Christian duties. They are compensated for by freedom from sin and by freedom from observing the prescriptions of the old law, henceforth outmoded by the economy of faith and the help of grace, always offered to those who ask for it with humility and confidence (cf. I Cor. 10.13). But today we should like to speak not so much of this happy asceticism, so worthy of our interest (cf. Eph. 6.17; I Thess. 5.8), as of the decline of a moral sense which characterizes our age. The very breadth of the theme obliges us to keep to just a few observations.

For example, can we exclude the sense of sin from our feelings about morality? Surely not, because sin has repercussions for our relationship with God. It is a fundamental truth of our ethical and religious conceptions; each one of our actions has a positive or negative effect on the order established by God in respect of us.

Now the radically lay mentality of our time annuls the first of our moral responsibilities, denying or neglecting the significance of our actions in respect of God, especially the negative consequences, that is to say, the offence caused to God by our sin.

Certainly the Christian should not resign himself to this bending of the present moral system. The whole economy of redemption is at stake.

Would it be enough to regard ourselves as being responsible only towards our own conscience? The moral conscience is certainly the proximate and indispensable criterion for judging the honesty of our actions.

Please God that the moral conscience will always benefit from the consideration which it deserves in the education of human beings. But the conscience has need of being instructed, trained and guided with respect to the objective good of the actions to be performed. The instinctive and intuitive judgment of the conscience is not enough. We need a norm and a law. Otherwise, judgment can alter under the pressure of passions, interests, or examples from elsewhere and moral life will live on utopias or instincts. And as we see today, it will become a moral life which bends to external circumstances and situations, with all the consequences of relativism and servilism which stem from that, even to the point of compromising the uprightness of conscience which we call character, and making men an oasis of 'reeds shaken by the wind' (Matt. 11.7).

You may hear it said that we must give our life a stamp of sincerity, and by sincerity what is meant here is the abandonment of man's personal liberty to his animal impulses, his ignoble egotism. You may hear it said today that the whole edifice of traditional morality is in course of collapsing because of the transformations of modern life, and that the criteria for our conduct must be anthropological and social, that is to say, that they must be conformity to current customs, without regard for the superior criteria of good and evil. And perhaps, even in Christian circles, you will see attacks on traditional belief in the natural law, the existence of which has even been disputed, and traditional belief in the magisterium of the church when this makes pronouncements in defence of the fundamental and sacred rights of a life which still deserves to be called human and Christian.

You will understand the ethical, social and political circumstances affected by the opposition between such a firm Christian morality and amoral permissiveness and provisional ethics. Think of the storm that is approaching our world! Think of the shipwreck in which our civilization may be engulfed!

You will understand that faithfulness to Christ, clearer than the *laissez-faire* attitude of so many people who call themselves Christians, must resume the guidance of our consciences. It is from baptism, which has regenerated us and made us children of God, that we draw as from their sources the norms and energies for the new life to which we have been called and which makes its demands on us.'

In this text, the Pope puts forward a certain number of key ideas summing up the morality of the church. He recalls the 'degrading currents of a secularized Christianity' and the existence of a 'movement of thought and action which is more impetuous than wise and which resembles 'ideas current in the world'. Without any doubt he condemns the 'agitation' of the ego represented by a youth looking for a standpoint in a world based on materialism, money and particularly harsh social competition (as one worker priest put it, you could see that he had never worked).

What does he propose as a basis for reflection?

1. The sense of sin; and he reminds us that each of our actions has a positive and a negative relationship with the order established by God with respect to us.

2. Observance of the law.

3. Obedience to the *magisterium* of the church.

4. A lack of confidence in man, whose conscience must be ceaselessly instructed, trained and guided.

5. The demands of rigorous asceticism imposed by the new Christian law (I was reminded of this text some years ago by a drop-out adolescent whom I shall call Hippie).

What is the true sense of the words of Christ which are quoted in this text? To deny oneself, to want to save one's life and to have to lose it in Christ's cause. Renunciation of self is indispensable for all psychological development; if it does not take place, a person risks remaining at a stage of narcissism, egocentricity and neurotic observance of the law. Is not an obsessive concern to save one's life the best way of losing it? Is not devoting one's life to love, communication, exchange, the best way of being happy? For that, is it necessary to be detached from external and temporal things, to exalt the poverty of the spirit, to offer the left cheek to anyone who strikes us on the right?

After a long medical practice I have increasing trust in man and his possibilities of growth. I do not believe that sincerity means 'abandoning man's personal liberty to his animal impulses, to his appetite for pleasure without superior inhibitions, to his ignoble egotism'.

Is there incompatibility between human flourishing, social success and Christian morality? Is it impossible to succeed in life by loving and respecting others? Is it not desirable that the church in our time should be more impetuous than wise, and that it should be seriously concerned with the ideas current in the world?

A national chaplain expressed his confusion at the fact that young people were leaving his movement. 'What do you do, Father,' I asked him, 'to enthuse them and win them over?' Their life is already difficult psychologically, and the absence of material problems is not a sign of happiness. They need people to have confidence in them; they need joy, love and enthusiasm. The time of traditional education which only teaches all the things we may not do is over. The rising generation is clear and courageous, and it wants to live in a different way. Society is changing rapidly. Rather than complain, we ought to think. Read this letter from a student of twenty-three whom I treated for three months. He had tried to commit suicide.

This civilization has done nothing for the fullness and development of the people who make it up: it has only invented a religion of work, and repeated in different ways the old neurotic image of original sin, with its fear of the body and the flesh. This civilization organizes life in terms of the division of work and production. It has brought about the most monstrous reversal possible by subjecting men to ideas constructed around a mythology of salvation and the beyond. . . Nietzsche talked about those 'hallucinated with the after-life', who only think of perverting in mankind the qualities which make us truly human. Christian civilization has arrived at a really stulted condition.

PART III

TOWARDS A NEW EDUCATION
AND A NEW CHURCH

7

The Education of Self-Love

Many people may find the title of this chapter equivocal. Steeped in traditional morality, they confuse self-love with egotism, the instinct for possession and the spirit of domination. They have become accustomed to the catchwords of Christian morality: 'Be concerned for others, do something for them, do not stay shut up in yourselves, do not think so much of yourselves, but think of those who need you. When you come out of your egotism, all your difficulties will disappear.'

Constraint, sacrifice, renunciation have never allowed the child and the adolescent to develop in harmony. It is necessary to have been able to give oneself to oneself before giving oneself to someone else. As Paul Valéry wrote, 'It is necessary to give value to what one is, as one is, whatever that may be.'

Contrary to what many people think, the egotist is not someone who loves himself. On the contrary, he hates himself. He cannot bear himself in the context in which he lives. He gathers everything to himself, wants to possess everything and have everything. But he cannot enjoy any of his possessions, does not dare to give himself to anything, and cannot conquer anything. He is never content with himself, perpetually shuns himself in search of a more satisfying image which will in fact never satisfy him. Sometimes this aggression against himself is disguised under the mask of an inordinate pride which puts those around him off the scent and deceives them (to be concerned with one's ego does not mean to relate everything to oneself). There is such a thing as a healthy egotism: that which allows someone to look at themselves in an objective way, without becoming infatuated, but also without belittling themselves and taking an excessively low view of themselves.

The healthy egoist is someone who can arrive at a certain estimation of himself, and who looks on himself with a degree of good will, not to mention a certain indulgence. He gets on well with himself. After twenty years in my profession, I have arrived at the conclusion that the happy ones are those who are pleased at themselves and who like their own company. Real happiness comes through love of oneself. The healthy egoist is a happy man who respects the independence of others.

People are such that it is evident that self-love is not as widespread as is commonly claimed. Many people are discontent with themselves and, perpetually unhappy, let off steam on those around them. Overwhelming them and criticizing everyone and everything, they promenade their peevishness and their aggressive judgment in search of a new foolish victim on whom they can pour scorn.

I have never met anyone who judges himself in a different way from that in which he judges others. Fundamentally, the person who criticizes his neighbour habitually criticizes himself or herself with just as much vigour. If one cannot accept oneself, one cannot accept others.

Love of self calls for a great deal of lucidity, objectivity and courage. To accept oneself is to accept communicating with oneself and to appreciate one's qualities and failings, one's potentialities and limitations. It is to succeed in living without being perpetually relative to someone else or to some rule or other which has been more or less well internalized. Finally, it is to accept being fully responsible for oneself, one's life and one's choices.

The education of self-love is diametrically opposed to traditional Christian education: it is based on confidence. In the collection 'The Pope speaks to You', there is a small volume entitled *The Pope Speaks to Youth*. In an address to the World Federation of Feminine Catholic Youth on 18 April 1952, Pius XII speaks of individual ethics and condemns the new ethics.

The new ethic, 'situation ethics', as these authors call it, is eminently individualistic. In determining his conscience, the individual has a direct encounter with God and makes up his mind before him, without the intervention of any law, any community, any cult or confession, in anyway whatsoever. Here there is only the 'I' of man and the 'I' of the personal God: not the God of the law but God the Father, with whom man is to unite in filial love.

From this perspective, then, the decision of conscience is a personal risk, depending on the knowledge and the evaluation of the individual, in all sincerity before God. These two things, right intention and sincere response, are what God takes into account. The action does not matter to him, to such an extent that the response can exchange the Catholic faith for other principles, leading to divorce, to an interruption of gestation, a refusal of obedience to the competent authority in the family, in the church, in the state. All that would be completely in accord with the condition of the majority of men and, in the Christian order, with the relationship of sonship which, according to the teaching of Christ, makes us pray "Our Father". This personal view spares man from having to ascertain at each moment whether the decision to be taken corresponds to the section of the law or the canon of norms and rules. It preserves him from the hypocrisy of a Pharisaic fidelity to the law; it preserves him from pathological scruples, whether these be shallow-mindedness or lack of confidence. It gives the Christian entire responsibility before God. That is the language of those who talk about the 'new morality'. This new ethic is so far behind Catholic faith and principles that even a child, if he knows his catechism, will note this and feel it. It is not difficult to recognize how the new moral system derives from existentialism, which either makes God into an abstraction or simply denies him, but in any case leaves man to himself.

If he is to be a whole person, is it not necessary for the Christian to feel responsible before God and for him to take a personal risk? This text follows the same lines as that of Paul VI on the decline of morality. Now the church does not have a monopoly in morality, and Christ came for all men of good will. I know many 'atheistic saints', free and responsible people who have no need of any law but that of respect for themselves and respect for others. I also know many Christians who, preoccupied with saving their souls, sprinkle their lives with charitable acts while remaining profoundly indifferent to others. The law is enough for them.

More than ever, the man of today knows that he must learn to think for himself, to reflect, to choose and to create. Nothing in this attitude is incompatible with the love of Christ. We live in a world which is changing everywhere. Automation, mechanization, industrialization, urbanization, the extraordinary development of modes of information and communication have broken up all the structures. People no longer live in homogeneous groups where their thought all follows the same norms, with the same convictions, and where they know clearly and certainly the nature of good and evil, what they should believe and what they should not, what they should accept and what they should reject. The barriers have disappeared, the walls and fortifications round our cities have vanished. We are thrown upon the world, steeped in a network of communications and multiple relations, confronted with ideas, cultures and beliefs alien to our own. When we lived together, we shared the same customs and felt the same way about things: we were agreed on ideas and principles. The stability, fixity and certainty of other days have been replaced with a permanent development and a dynamism: everything is constantly put in question. Our judgments cannot be categorical and definitive any more; they must become more relative, with a certain coefficient of probability which threatens our peace of mind. We can no longer allow ourselves to make categorical instant judgments. We can only understand and interpret in a perspective, a history, in terms of what has gone before and what will come after.

How can we change a world that we do not accept? How can we accept earthly life if we have to scorn it to deserve eternal life? It is much more difficult to educate children and adolescents in such a way as to make them free and responsible people than to impose on them a fixed morality which will train them to follow the directives of the Holy Father in everything.

Education in self-love begins at birth. It imposes two imperatives on parents.

First, inculcating in the child a love of life, leaving it the possibility of undergoing an apprenticeship in sexual pleasure through the satisfaction of its drives. In fact, to use rigorous prohibition to prevent a child from eating sweets, dirtying itself, being cruel or masturbating, contributes to an exaggerated development of the idea of sin and risks inhibiting completely its further psychological and sexual growth.

Second, allowing the child, through the frustrations inherent in any education, to come to sense its own responsibilities. It is wrong to think that children must be allowed everything. Prohibition and the limitation of pleasure are necessary for intellectual investment and social and cultural development. As far as education goes, the child feels prohibitions to be a limitation of its freedom, but also to be a defence against its instincts, in the shelter of which it can better shape itself and develop. However, the child will only accept its first frustrations if it has a deep sense of its mother's love. The mother must not just feed it, but look after it and arouse in it some pleasant or unpleasant physical sensations. Thanks to the care which she lavishes on it, she becomes its first seducer. From the oral phase onwards, the mother acquires a unique importance, and for the two sexes becomes the object of the first and most powerful of loves, the prototype of all subsequent loving relationships.

What matters more than anything is the emotional climate in which the baby lives. From the eighth month on, it begins to distinguish the face of its mother from other faces and is evidently anxious whenever the mother is away. It interprets maternal attitudes as so many emotional signals. An attitude of refusal or rejection often makes the child apathetic, with difficulty in sleeping and digestive troubles (vomiting and anorexia). An excessively protective and anxious attitude can induce in it agitated behaviour, which represents a permanent lack of satisfaction and which can be maintained by increasingly tyrannical demands. If the mother's moods are variable, the child responds by a physical and psychological instability which in fact represents a feeling of insecurity. In the case of conflict between mother and child, when the baby is deprived of care and caresses, serious troubles appear, like failure to put on weight, a halt to intellectual development, and problems of character which will prevent the future adult from making normal emotional ties.

In the course of this education, in which love is the chief element, the baby's desire is changed and takes on an emotional colouring. To begin with, this is the satisfaction of a physiological function. Secondarily, it becomes a need for the emotional presence of the mother. The relationship then develops in a new dimension. While the need for milk is satisfied and disappears, the need for the mother's presence never disappears. This mother who both cherishes her child and frustrates it by her absence is both loved and hated. She causes its greatest joys and its deepest sufferings.

Progressively, the child arranges its defences and turns the exclusive attention devoted to its mother towards other sources of interest: its own body and the outside world. It discovers autoerotic activities which alleviate its anxiety: it caresses its lips, the contours of its mouth, moves its tongue in a way reminiscent of sucking, and puts a finger in its mouth. Sucking the thumb symbolizes union with the absent mother. The thumb is a kind of substitute for the breast. Soon, this activity is projected outwards and the baby catches hold of a piece of blanket, a rattle, a brick, which it puts in its mouth. From that point on, through play and ceaseless experimenting, by exploring with its mouth, of which it knows all the nuances, the child differentiates external objects.

During the anal phase, the mother must allow the baby to bear with the frustrations inherent in learning to control the sphincter. At this stage, the child takes great pleasure in retaining or releasing its faeces in accordance with its fantasies. Aware of its mother's anxiety in this respect, the child manipulates its faeces like a magical object: part of its own body, it models them at will in the course of games which have no element of disgust in them. At a second stage it trades them off against the affection of its mother and the assurance of a satisfactory relationship. In this perspective they acquire the value of a gift. From the moment it achieves control of the sphincter, the child becomes capable of affirming its independence and resisting pressure.

Rigid and perfectionist mothers are dangerous for babies. They do not give them time to develop harmoniously. I remember a conversation with the mother of a young man of twenty, suffering from schizophrenia. I asked her about the early childhood of her son.

'I assure you, doctor, he was perfect. He gave me no trouble. He was clean at one year old' (a child brought up normally is clean about the age of two).

'At what age did you put him on the pot?'

'I remember very clearly. It was towards six months, I believe.' (One should wait until nine or ten months.) 'He was clean before his two small cousins of the same age. He was always very advanced. He made his first communion at nine and got his certificate in higher maths at fifteen, with a "good".'

'And at eighteen he fell ill.'

'Yes, it's incomprehensible. In the sixth form his prefect (the person in charge of classes in a free school) said to me: Your son is an example to his fellow pupils, he is quite above reproach.'

I treated the young man for five years. It would take too long to tell his story, but he is now cured. At the beginning of his illness he would spend hours in the lavatory cleaning himself in case he was soiled in any way. I soon broke with the mother, who could not accept that her son was no longer attached to her.

This great Christian (she made her communion every morning), apparently kind and charitable, was in fact proud and intolerant. She wore her son in her buttonhole like the Legion of Honour.

From its earliest age, the child needs love, recognition and respect for its needs if its psychological development is to be normal. Later, from the time of puberty and adolescence, a ready ear, tolerance and love remain the basis of education. Many uneducated parents think that their children are too fond of themselves. That is a mistake. Far from loving themselves too much, they very often have powerful feelings of inferiority and guilt which are reinforced by moralizing judgments. How many times have I heard parents say of their child: 'Doctor, I can't do anything with this child; he is unbearable, he won't work, he is absent-minded and insolent, he talks back to everyone and you have to keep telling him the same thing; in class and at home he never stops acting the fool, to draw attention to himself. Sometimes he even steals and tells lies. The whole problem is that he thinks of nothing but himself. If he had been an only child, that would have been all very well, but he cannot bear his brothers and sisters, and is always demanding attention. He's never concerned about others. You should advise him to be interested in something, to think how he could help out at home and be a little less preoccupied with himself.'

When one actually sees the child, it is clear that this boy who shows off, is insolent, contradicts, does all this only because he is infinitely doubtful about himself, constantly plays himself down and cannot accept himself for what he is. He ceaselessly criticizes himself, mistrusts himself and then can only criticize, mistrust and reject others. When one asks these young people to write their failings on one side of a sheet of paper and their good qualities on the other, one is astonished to note the ease with which they fill the column for their failings. It is rare that they find one or two good qualities, and then not without giving the impression of being at fault, of lying and deceiving those who are questioning them. For them it is a real liberation when they are told that they do not know how to love, that they have the right to satisfaction, the right to love existence, that perhaps they can make a little less effort, let themselves go a bit, and then things will not prove to be too bad.

Oldest sons are often the most affected: too much is required of them too quickly. That is for two reasons: first, the lack of know-how on the part of young parents (they become much more philosophical over the second child and subsequent children). And the birth of the second child pushes the first one forward and too quickly gives him senior status.

A young man of twenty-one came to see me by himself. He had left his family the year before and was living in a rural community. He had been a deserter for two months.

'I didn't reply to the call-up papers I received in September: my father handed them to me with the words, "Cheer up, the army will make you a responsible man." '

'What does your father do?'

'He is an administrator at the Finance Ministry.'

'Why did you leave your family?'

'I couldn't bear either my brothers and sisters or my parents. My father kept telling me I was setting a bad example.'

'What were you doing?'

'Nothing. That's the problem. I passed my school-leaving examination three years ago. I got a "good" in maths. The superior advised my parents to "put me" in advanced maths.'

'You didn't agree?'

'No one asked me what I thought. I wanted to do photography and the cinema. My father demanded that I should first do serious study. I did senior maths for two years. I left home after the first term of special maths. The atmosphere had become intolerable. Every evening, over supper, in front of everyone, my father kept criticizing me. "Don't follow the example of your older brother. He's got no will power. He'll get the dunce's cap," and so on.'

'Did your father make great demands on you?'

'Yes, and my mother even more so. She wanted me to be perfect. I had no right to get bad marks. She was much more indulgent towards the others. From the fourth year on I forged my reports to avoid being told off. I was never allowed to smoke at home or to go into a night club, so that I wouldn't set a bad example. The friends I brought home were never good enough. "Think," my mother told me, "that these boys could be your sisters' husbands." When I went to the cinema I had to take my sister and my brother with me; they were two and four years younger than I. If I refused, I was told that I was selfish. My father often reminded me of the material difficulties that he had at my age. My grandfather was a postman. He was promoted within the post office and worked very hard. After I left home I received several letters from my mother. She begged me to return, because she was afraid that my example might be contagious.'

'What do you want to do?'

'Go home, no question about it.'

'For military service?'

'I'm afraid of that. When I got my call-up papers, I didn't sleep for several days.'

'Why?'

'I was afraid of facing a world I didn't know. I no longer know where I am. I'm anxious and I brood all day. Basically, I'm not much good. Now, I'm obsessed with the fear of going to prison.'

'What do you do in the community where you now live?'

'I keep busy gardening and cooking. I'm incapable of doing anything else. I try to read, but I can't concentrate.'

Some days after this conversation, I had the young man admitted to hospital so that he could have a complete examination. I had found him depressed and generally in a bad state. The examination confirmed my first impression. Blood tests revealed anaemia and an abnormal count of white cells. The psychological examination confirmed the magnitude of the depression, with a clear deterioration in intellectual potential. I sent him with his notes to the military hospital at Val-de-Grâce, and several weeks afterwards he was discharged.

When he left hospital he did not go home. He took part-time work and prepared for the school of photography at Vaugirard. He remained depressed for several months. This young man who had left an apparently well-structured family, loving and well-disposed, was thought by many people to be a hothead. His desertion didn't help: a priest to whom I spoke about his case said, 'These young men must learn to bend their backs.' In fact this young man had run away from his surroundings to try to survive. Made to feel completely useless and guilty, he had no faith in himself.

His father came to see me.

'Doctor,' he said, 'I know Philippe very well. He's leading you up the garden path. He has never been able to bear the presence of his brothers and sisters. He is selfish, lazy, and a liar. He wanted to be discharged. He got what he wanted. He refuses to see me because he knows that I am not deceived by these farcical goings-on.'

'Forgive me, but I don't agree with you. You don't know your son at all. He loves his brothers and sisters, and has a great deal of admiration and affection for you. He left because he could not bear not to be able to keep up with your demands. As for his discharge, it was fully justified. Several times a year I see parents who come to see me, devastated after the suicide of one of their children. It is dangerous to press a depressed adolescent too hard. Philippe is now regaining his balance. He is regaining confidence in himself. Soon, I think, he will be asking to see you. When that happens, let him speak, listen to him; he needs your understanding and your respect.'

'I hope, doctor, that you're not barking up the wrong tree.'

'Have confidence in Philippe and you won't regret it.'

The incredulous and suspicious attitude of this 'father full of good will' was contradicted by the warm handshake which he gave me as he left.

Philippe succeeded in getting into the school at Vaugirard at the first attempt. He was enthusiastic about his studies and he seems to have found his calling. With his friends, he has just made a film in Super 8 called *The Deserter*. I'm impatiently waiting for the first showing.

Our moralizing reaction is even more dangerous towards skinheads, punks, mods, teddy boys, indeed any young people who seem to have rejected all constraints and to give free course to their instincts. They seem beyond the reach of all moral rules. It is necessary to discover what really moves them, the real motivations for their criminal and morally reprehensible conduct. In fact they behave in such a way that they give themselves a certain idea and a certain image of themselves. Basically, these are young men and women who have a low opinion of themselves and try to compensate in many ways for their feelings of inferiority and helplessness. By satisfying instincts in a way which is always deceptive, they try to avoid anxiety and rid themselves of their guilt-feelings. The best attitude is to understand them and accept them, to reassure them about their unhappiness, to give them the possibility of expressing themselves and arouse in them the idea of self-respect, telling them that despite everything they have the right and even the duty to love themselves.

Being romantics, adolescents dream of absolutes. They find it very difficult to accept the relativity of existence, of love and of their own reality. Many cherish dreams of love in which the other person in the last resort has little substance. The other is only the imaginary projection of their desire for the absolute, the dream which compensates for the unacceptable bankruptcy of reality. They dream of perfect communion and absolute happiness. This is the myth of Tristan and Isolde, a passion which can be fulfilled only in death. Only the love of parents or those who teach them, their understanding, the dealings which parents or teachers have with young people, can allow them to overcome this obstacle, the failure of this illusion, becoming more truly aware of what they are and what other people are. It is by the acceptance of failure that they become people and become human. It is by identification with adults whom they accept and recognize that they evolve towards autonomy and learn a sense of relativity.

Unfortunately many adults have not gone beyond the stage of

adolescent emotions. They are always tempted to escape from relativity in the illusory quest for a perfect and absolute relationship in which there will be total communication without any distinction between the self and the other person, and this void, this gulf, this sensation of loss and dissatisfaction felt by those who do not love themselves, is done away with. In his book *Love and the West*, Denis de Rougemont gives a good demonstration of the nature of this passionate love: the obstacle, the absence, whatever it is which makes the sought-for union impossible. Pain becomes a pleasure, pleasure is sought in suffering, and finds its most intense pressure in the approach of death, almost desired as the supreme pleasure. Many immature adults continue to dream of an imaginary and idealized love and are incapable of accepting reality, which is both acceptance of pleasure and acceptance of frustration.

The personality can be formed only through the acceptance of pleasure and the renunciation of this pleasure. A mother said to me, 'I have never caressed my child, I have never much wanted to take him in my arms, to kiss him, because at a later stage I wanted him to have only intellectual needs; the pleasures of the senses can only lead to deceit and suffering.' This mother did not allow her child to know the security and the stability which are the only things which make it possible to accept the inescapable frustrations of existence. Many difficult adolescents and many unbalanced grown-ups have been children who were not given enough love. All through their life they retain a feeling of not being wanted, and they are always in search of a love which they cannot find. They do not love themselves and are persuaded that no one can love them.

How can the adolescent accept the necessary frustrations and renunciations?

One of the most important periods in the education of self-love is the Oedipal period. The boy must renounce the love he has for his mother and accept his father as a rival. The girl must renounce the love she knows for her father and accept the mother as a rival. For the child, this renunciation is possible only through identification, that is to say, the acceptance of the parental images offered to it. At this period education is particularly difficult; excessively weak and indulgent parents favour the formation of an excessively severe superego of a masochistic kind, the child imposing on itself the most cruel prohibitions, which can range from chastity to the most monastic kind of asceticism. Harsh and demanding parents will prevent the child's superego from developing. He or she will become a weak and disabled adult, incapable of making existential choices.

The role of good parents, if they exist, is thankless and difficult. It consists in not going too far in one direction or the other. Educators must be catalysts and not trainers. Our moralizing reflexes can only irritate the adolescent in search of himself. Many parents remind me of those grossly overweight doctors who want their patients to go on a diet: 'Do as I tell you. . .'

Incessant judgments, lack of confidence, prevent the adolescent from feeling accepted and likewise from accepting himself or herself. Education must allow them to adapt by resolving the conflicts between what we call the pleasure-principle and the reality-principle. In its brute state, instinct is guided by the pleasure-principle; instinctual drives demand the immediate satisfaction of the need which secures relaxation and pleasure. But this pleasure-principle very soon comes up against the reality-principle, in the sense that the immediate and total satisfaction of the needs is materially impossible. It is by means of a series of successive frustrations that the child and the adolescent become aware of the resistance from the external world. Little by little they learn a sense of relativity. They discover that there is no precise frontier between good and evil, between vice and virtue, between success and failure. There is something of failure in success and something of success in failure, just as there is something of night in the day and something of day in the night. There is not normality on one hand and a pathological state on the other; a natural side and a supernatural side; myself on one side confronted with the other. There is a dialectical and living relationship which makes them interpenetrate without becoming confused. By means of personal experience the adolescent will accept that pleasure is never total, that satisfaction is never absolute and that perfection does not exist. He knows that to accept life he must accept death; to accept pleasure he must accept renunciation. He will learn the apparently paradoxical dialectic of existence, namely that one cannot love the other without loving oneself, that one cannot take without giving nor possess without being obliged to give oneself. Thus this 'child-object', whose needs express themselves more than he or she expresses them, will progressively become an 'adult-subject' who, by agreeing to subordinate the pleasure-principle to the reality-principle, will succeed in mastering the relationship which binds him to the world and distinguish times for satisfaction. He will construct his own moral conscience without being perpetually relative to the other, or to some law which systematically constrains him.

A girl of about eighteen whom I was treating for an anxiety neurosis said to me at one of our last meetings,

'You have taught me to look with my eyes and really to see the world around me. You have also taught me to see with the eyes of others.'

'What do you mean?'

'When I came to see you I was afraid of everything. I always felt guilty, and that other people were judging me. I kept repeating what was often said to me by the Superior of the institution in which I was brought up: "What doesn't cost anything doesn't lead to much." Tense and dissatisfied, I tried ceaselessly to achieve perfection. Since I underwent psychotherapy I have learnt that my education was artificial and abnormal. It is impossible to spend one's life trying to be like the Virgin Mary, St Thérèse of the Child Jesus, and all the saints of paradise. One day or another you will crack, as did the splendid Superior I mentioned to you. (After a nervous breakdown, she left orders.) Possessed by this teaching about the absolute, I did not exist outside my good actions and my charitable deeds. At all costs I wanted to be loved by everyone and hear them say, "Look how well brought up that girl is, kind and loving." I lived through the judgments and the assessments of others. I began to accept myself and to have confidence in what I felt, what I believed and what I thought. I no longer asked what so and so might have done in my place. The most astonishing thing is that before this change I thought that I was open and loving. In fact I was intolerant and aggressive. I had the truth, and in the name of this truth I condemned in my mind all those who did not think as I did.'

'What do you mean by "seeing with the eyes of others"?'

'I learned a sense of relativity. I came to understand that we are conditioned by our education, our way of life, our cultural setting. My relationships with others have changed completely. I am eager to discover them. I now know what it means not to be self-centred. I like to discuss with people who don't think as I do. I try to put myself in their place and understand their point of view. I have the impression of having been blind and deaf, shut up in an infernal world in which communication no longer exists. Dialogue with others has replaced my obsessive interior dialogue.'

This girl has kept her religious convictions. She is part of a group of students studying the basis of a new spirituality and is busy with Catholic Action in the business school which she entered this year.

Education must be based on dialogue and communication. But what is the exact meaning of these terms which many people use without knowing precisely what they signify? Communication is first of all a matter of listening and understanding what the other person says, what he believes, what he thinks. It is also a matter of saying what we are, what we think, what we believe. All true communication is based on the respect and the love of the other person, on the respect and love of ourselves. It allows us to abandon the immature attitude which allows only for consideration of its own point of view. It is a matter of learning to make the effort to listen and to make oneself understood. It implies constant reciprocity and self-involvement. One cannot maintain this relationship with others without constant self-analysis, and it is a relationship which demands that one sheds a maximum of light in communication with oneself. By virtue of this it is a living demand which puts our own authority in question. It calls for going beyond the sign and understanding the sign, towards a signification and an open symbolism. Self-love and the love of others come together and allow each one to ensure his or her own being, own time and own responsibility.

8

The Church, an Assembly of the People?

For twenty years I have been in permanent contact with Catholic or Protestant Christians, priests, religious, bishops and pastors. One thing has always struck me: despite appearances of stability and immobility, the church has never ceased to be the scene of an intensive upheaval. There is an ebb and flow; ideas grow, spread and withdraw, even seem to disappear, and then are reborn in a better form some years, or some centuries later.

In recent years, grass-roots communities and charismatic groups have been multiplying all over the world with different nuances, in a way which seems unstoppable. These new structures are developing at the very moment when people are complaining about the crisis in the parishes, the crisis in recruitment to the priesthood, the crisis of faith and secularization.

It is important to make a distinction between grass-roots communities, which are usually formed in an atmosphere of conflict with the established church, and charismatic groups, which are founded on a rediscovery of prayer and accept the system of the church as it is. What they have in common is that they have not been imposed from above by the hierarchy. They come from the grass roots, from the people of God, which rediscovers itself among them, because it can express itself there, pray there and live there in a framework of freedom which is a real liberation in comparison with everything which seemed fixed and immobile. They experiment with a new type of community life and structure which makes light of geographical settings, social milieux, race and even culture. These Christians are aware of being the church as they gather together in the name of Jesus Christ and bear witness in their manner of living. Formed spontaneously, these communities have no administrative super-structure. They give an equal welcome to priests, bishops, lay, religious, members of other churches and non-believers, these last coming to experience for the first time who Jesus Christ is. This non-hierarchical structure naturally finds a place within both communities and groups: it is based on experience of life, prayer and each member's particular gifts.

To understand the extent of this phenomenon one has to have been to an assembly like that held in Rennes in 1972 for French grass-roots communities, or to the convention which met in the USA in June 1973, which drew 23,000 charismatic Catholics.

There are upwards of four hundred grass-roots communities in France. Membership numbers between ten and thirty; all are on first-name terms, and between them there is an exceptional human warmth which allows for sharing and having things in common. Some communities represent a radical break with the church, and are completely peripheral. The majority are in a situation of 'conflictual solidarity' or are indifferent towards the traditional parish. Most often these are urban, and are made up of former militants of Catholic Action or student groups, and depend either on a sympathetic priest or on religious who live in the same district or the same locality. For most of the time the members of these communities are involved in politics, either in trade unions or in local government. They represent a strong force in the country. They meet several times a month in a hall belonging to a society or to the community. They discuss and eat together, and their meetings take place in an atmosphere of joy. The meal is often linked with a domestic eucharist. In exceptional cases this has been celebrated without a priest.

While feeling that the distinction between the priest and the laity is finished, the members of these grass-roots communities think that the priest is the 'minister of unity with the universal church, to the degree that he has the confidence of the bishop and also that of the community'. They would not do away with the specific character of the priestly ministry, but 'there is no reason why the minister should be celibate, male, or hold the position permanently'. They think that priests must emerge from communities and be accepted by the hierarchies.

These communities are autonomous and self-supporting, materially and spiritually, but they do not deny the need for more general church structures. They think that those which exist at present are ineffective, are no longer capable of renewing themselves or of raising up new ministers for which the people of God feels a deep need. This reaction is a sign of a modification in collective thought which has affected the whole of society: the erosion of patriarchal society and the refusal to accept imposed authority. The people wants to be able to choose its officials, those who guide its life and thought. This is a general fact, whether or not the hierarchy accepts it. It is no longer enough to be invested with the attributes of authority, power, or even knowledge, to make oneself felt. This development can be seen at the level of the family group, the university, the church and the working world. There will no longer be a teaching church and a taught church, but one single church, living and dynamic, in which lay participation will become more and more important. In many respects this adventure is as exciting as that undertaken by the first community in Jerusalem and the first disciples of Francis of Assisi. The present-day church must agree to 'die to itself', losing its neurotic structure and its overwhelming superego, if it wants to regain contact with today's world. The Roman authorities find themselves confronted with the problem of universal suffrage and autonomy. Some years ago a theologian explained to me that the present imbalance in the church in fact derives from the Middle Ages. The very important development of the cult of the dead necessitated the ordination of a large number of 'altar' priests (i.e. priests dedicated to the altar), whose sole function was to say mass. Thus the clergy occupied too important a place at the heart of the church, and gradually the priests took over all social and human activities. It is now to be desired that the number of priests should decrease and that lay people should have greater responsibility in the Christian community (for example, as deacons). Through this spontaneous development among the people of God, the church might perhaps rediscover its equilibrium.

In contrast to grass-roots communities, charismatic groups do not claim to have any critical function. They have the experience of renewed Pentecost, and increasingly seem to be a church without boundaries. Catholic Pentecostalism was born in the United States in 1966, at Duquesne University in Pittsburgh and the University of Notre Dame in Indiana. In these groups Christians relived in an overpowering way what is written in the Acts of the Apostles and in particular in the letters of Paul. The Holy Spirit, received through the sacraments of baptism and confirmation, was in some way reactivated by prayer and the laying on of hands, to such an extent that people experienced a real 'outpouring of the Spirit' which manifested itself in prayer, in speaking in unknown languages, gifts of prophecy, healing, and so on. These meetings were devoted to prayer and the praise of God. Prayer was rediscovered as a joy which does away with time. It was offered either spontaneously or with the help of the Bible. It developed in several stages: prayer, teaching, eucharist, preparation of those who wanted to receive the spirit. These groups welcome anyone, and have to multiply rapidly to keep within reasonable bounds. Cures are by no means rare. Public confession of sins, with thanks to God for his forgiveness, presents no problem. . .The person in charge of the group (maybe a young girl, maybe the father of a family), makes sure that limits are not overstepped. Obviously there is a risk of abuse and collective hysteria.

This movement has spread like a tidal wave. In the United States there are more than 1,200 groups, and in France, fifty have emerged in less than a year. At the Notre Dame convention, thirty countries were represented, with twenty-two members from France. There are charismatic groups in the fourteen Trappist monasteries in the United States. The movement has an episcopal counsellor and about a dozen bishops have already joined it. 750 priests concelebrated at the closing mass of the convention, at which Cardinal Suenens, won-over and enthusiastic, preached a sermon in which Paul VI was acclaimed every time his name was mentioned.

The grass-roots communities and the charismatic groups are two indications of the vitality of the people of God. I have been struck by the attitude of several members of the hierarchy, who find the grass-roots communities suspicious because they criticize traditional structures and claim the right to share in the nomination of priests; they are truly groups which reflect on and research into new ways of living, new modes of involving the priest and new conditions of the ordained ministry. It is not impossible to reconcile these two apparently opposed attitudes. The time will come when the communities will be able to present one of their members for the priesthood, but it will always be the bishop who makes the choice and calls the person in the name of the church.

There is much less reticence towards charismatic groups. The traditional church has no objections. It seems quite favourable to the development of this movement based on prayer and the experience of the presence of the Holy Spirit, which appeals solely to emotion and involvement, not to critical reason and reflection. Let me recall the reply of the sociology student who came back from the USA having shared in this kind of meeting. 'I remained something of a spectator. I didn't succeed in belonging to that kind of gut religion, with its collective hysteria.' His criticism might seem somewhat severe. However, it does seem that too many people risk being attracted by the miraculous aspect. The 'tongues' of which people speak are made up of 'almost unknown dialects, coming from areas into which Christianity has never penetrated'. Might this not be very elementary onomatopoeic jargon. . .? I wish the participants would suddenly start talking in Russian or Chinese. All the Christian intellectuals with whom I have talked about this maintain a prudent reserve.

The aspect of 'miracle and healing' is much more banal, above all in America, where the masses very rapidly get excited at spectacular and collective methods of healing. The 'transactional analysis' preached by Thomas Harris, the Sacramento psychiatrist, seems to me to have a great deal of similarity to our old Coué method. This form of treatment has spread with such success that a pastor in charge of a training institute for transactional analysis declared that 'Thomas Harris has done for psychotherapy what Henry Ford did for the automobile!' I personally feel incapable of giving a medical opinion on miracles witnessed to by charismatic groups. However, the very positive side of the charismatic movement, which accepts the church's system as it is, is without doubt the rediscovery of collective prayer and its ecumenical aspect.

The French Catholic Association for the Study of the Bible devoted its last Congress, in Lille, to the healing miracles recorded in the gospels. A hundred and sixty people, including some members of Anglican and Protestant confessions, shared in this work. This association thinks that the gospel accounts of miracle cannot be read naively if one takes seriously the problems which the contemporary specialists raise in connection with them. Taking particular accounts as starting points, each member of the conference developed a method applicable to these texts. I am impatiently awaiting the publication of their research, and I hope that this association will be interested in miracle, to which charismatic prayer groups bear witness.

Be this as it may, these new faces of the church, unimaginable fifteen years ago, are important signs of which we must take account. As one bishop said: 'If they are of God, they will bear fruit. From now on they give the church and Christians much to think about, and they contribute to a reassessment of the routines and structures which life seems to have left behind.'

9

Adam and Abraham

Referring to the Bible, the American sociologist Frederick Herzberg, one of the pioneers of job enrichment, sees the nature of man under two aspects. There is the animal who seeks security and wants to avoid all pain and all bother. This is represented by Adam, symbol of the alienated man who seeks to avoid all suffering. On the other hand, however, we discover an intelligent and sensitive being who desires to develop, to go beyond himself and to flourish. This sensitive man has been associated by Herzberg with Abraham, the elect of God, who shows his capacity to become what he is, to flourish: this is no longer the man determined by the drives which go beyond him, but the man who is master of his destiny. Is it not the role of the church to help people evolve from the Adam stage to the Abraham stage? In this connection I recall a discussion with a Benedictine who came to consult me over asthmatic attacks. In the course of one of our conversations we discussed at his request the formation of the ego and the superego. I expressed the idea that classical Christian education prevented man from developing a flexible and autonomous superego, capable of adapting itself.

'Doctor,' he told me, 'your idea is a dangerous one. It allows all kinds of abuses and laxities. Man needs an authority, a law, a father. The reference to the father is indispensable, i.e. obedience to a divine law. Christ took human form, but always did the will of his Father. Every Christian must be anxious; he must constantly ask himself, what does he want of me?'

'What a situation! I can see in it all the ideas of Paul VI. Man is treated as a being in search of security whom the church regards as a child, perpetually subjecting him to a law external to himself: he cannot be trusted.'

'He can be trusted to the extent that he obeys the law.'

'He can be trusted – just that. The superego must be allowed to construct itself, internalizing at a deep level everything that education brings it. During the crisis of adolescence, the young person questions everything. He constructs himself from within, having been first constructed from the outside, by the family, the school, the church. He needs to redigest everything, to reassimilate everything. An education based on obedience and obliteration does not allow this crisis, and by the same token, does not allow the superego to develop.'

'Yes, perhaps you're right. When I think of my novitiate . . . that was shattering. I remember a novice who rebelled constantly. I think he had a deep faith and a real vocation, but he was incapable of bending to the rule imposed on him. He was advised to leave.'

'A living faith calls for free adherence, deep and creative, and based on inner demands. If it is imposed and static, it does not allow of free growth.'

'I like your expression "build oneself up from within". In fact we are constructed from outside, and that is why we constantly seek to reassure ourselves. . . I came to see you because I'm constantly anxious. I think that my asthma is largely due to this anxiety.'

'When did it begin?'

'Two years ago.'

'What happened two or three years ago?'

'I can't think of anything important. . . We had a change of Prior three years ago. This change was caused by financial difficulties. We had an overdraft of hundreds of thousands of francs at the bank. Under the prompting of the new Prior, the community decided to open a youth centre. I was put in charge of organizing this centre.'

'Did you find it difficult to take on this responsibility?'

'Yes, I always felt that I would fail.'

'Why? Did you perhaps lack training?'

'Completely. I was put in charge for the sole reason that the community thought that I was the person.'

'On what criteria?'

'I seem to be a person who gives the impression of being calm and organized. In fact I'm neither. I'm introspective and meticulous to the point of obsession. I need a closed, well-ordered universe. Suddenly I was brought face to face with an open world in which order is ceaselessly overturned. A youth centre is difficult to organize.'

'Do you think that your asthma was caused by this psychological tension?'

'It's possible. It began gradually. I used to wake up in the night, finding it hard to breathe. The local doctor gave me some tranquillizers. Last winter I had influenza. It was at the end of that influenza that I got my first asthmatic attack. Now I have several a week.'

'Have they left you in charge?'

'Yes, but they've given me an assistant.'

'Would you like to be completely relieved of the directorship of this centre?'

'Yes and no. . . I don't think I should let myself take refuge in sickness.'

'Would your Prior agree to your accepting psychotherapy?'

'I haven't talked to him about it. He agreed that I should come to see you. I think that he will accept the treatment which you have prescribed for me.'

'I think that you have to pass from the Adam stage to the Abraham stage.'

'What do you mean?'

'You are a person built up from outside, with reference to norms and laws which have either not been internalized or have been internalized badly. Your superego is fragile, which explains your repression and your obsessional meticulousness. Your superego cannot cope with the "job enrichment" which has been proposed to you. You have to cope with work, responsibility, an atmosphere with which you are unfamiliar. You find difficulty in adapting, which explains your anxiety and the difficulties you have in assuming this new task. Your asthma is probably due to the introversion of this anxiety. Adam is a very feeble being who is seeking to avoid all anxiety and all responsibility. By contrast, Abraham is a being who seeks to realize himself, to blossom out, one might say to structure himself, in order to become autonomous and a master of himself.'

With the agreement of his superior, this religious is now undergoing a course of relaxation and psychotherapy. He continues to be responsible for his centre. A suitable course in chemotherapy has made his asthmatic attacks disappear, and that allows him to develop without being tempted to regress or take refuge in his sickness. It is worth noting that he has never questioned his vocation.

That is not always the case. Many priests I have looked after do precisely that. They have the feeling that they have been 'taken for a ride'. An assistant general of a secular order told me that he was fighting for the novitiate to refuse to accept young men of seventeen and eighteen: he had the feeling that their enthusiasm was being taken advantage of and that they would go directly from a religious school and a traditional Christian family to a religious novitiate or a major seminary . . . without having had 'time to form themselves'. He told me:

'To become a priest or a religious, people must be able to "stand up from within".'

The church, like present-day society, finds itself faced with the problems of job enrichment, that is to say the permanent training and the psychological, professional and cultural education of its priests. A priest of about thirty said to me,

'I feel incapable of continuing to do the same work all my life. I have the feeling that I am a dispenser of sacraments. In the large urban parish where I have been a curate for two years I spend my time baptizing, hearing confessions and marrying.'

'Do you do no work with young people?'

'Youth movements are becoming increasingly rare. In the parish the scout movement has disappeared for lack of leaders.'

'But plenty of people come to see you. Perhaps they are helped by your listening to them.'

'I don't think that listening is enough. I've no psychological training. I avoid giving advice. I always want to tell them, "Think, make a choice, take your own decisions." '

'That's not at all bad.'

'I feel incapable of being a reassuring father-image and the traditional spiritual director.'

'Why?'

'I don't think that that is the priest's role. I had a spiritual director who always said to me, "Think about the problems and come and tell me when you've made a decision." '

'Didn't this reply seem valuable to you?'

'Yes, but I know that what the faithful want of me above all else is reassurance. I cannot bear confession, above all on the eves of festivals. The worst of the parish arrive at the last moment and one has to hear in succession whole litanies of sins.'

'But doesn't the sacrament of penance have a liberating role all the same?'

'For the moment, yes. But on the eves of festivals I see the same people coming back, young or old, to repeat the same thing to me. . .'

'They're going round in circles.'

'And I have the impression that I'm not being any help to them. I would like to be a catalyst, helping Christians to reflect on their faith, their family attitude, their action in society. I would like to do something in youth work. I teach the catechism. . .'

There again, there is much to say. We have no other training but this: repetition=knowledge, knowledge=faith. In a lecture given at the last conference of the International Catholic Office of the Child, Père Girardi argued that Catholic teaching integrates the child into existing society instead of liberating him and allowing him to be part of a new society.

While Christians remain alienated people, the clerical structure will survive in its present form. Unfortunately for it, the younger generation wants to develop and become responsible, masters of their destiny. They will no longer accept being Adam. They want to become Abraham. Between these two men there is all the dynamism and growth which leads to the liberty of being and judging and rejects a legalistic morality based on doubt and mistrust.

10

'Decolonizing' the Child

For centuries the church has devoted a great deal of its time and energy to education. Paradoxically, we might note that while in society the crisis in education forces adults more and more to ask about the status of childhood and to experiment with new forms of education, many priests and sisters are turning away from this sector to discover the world of work and to throw themselves, as they say, into the real working world. Of those who remain in work with children, a large number justify their involvement less by love of youth than by a concern to reach parents through their children.

To be a catechist today is surely one of the most difficult of tasks. This difficulty is due to the crisis in education and the problem raised by the very content of the faith. Is it really necessary to base the catechism on the school system, and teach a child the essentials of the faith before the age of thirteen? In the journal *Catéchistes*, Jean Babin writes:

> People have wanted to change everything, methods and language, but what is really needed is a fundamental change in structure. In fact we have invested our resources in teaching the catechism to young people of sixteen to eighteen, following school age. Now we know that psychologically the most effective periods for catechism are up to the age of six and then from the ages of eighteen to thirty.

On the other hand, is it possible to transmit, to hand on, such a personal experience as faith? How can a traditional Christian milieu which experiences its religion as a rule have an educational role? As one of the teachers in a Christian school said to me, the 'cult of the rule' has never helped anyone to progress.

Many children have a growing need to receive direct answers to their questions about the meaning of life and death. The magazine *Okapi*, published by Bayard Press and aimed at children from eight to eleven, recently asked its readers what interested them and what questions they ask about life and God. More than two thousand children replied. Here are the questions that they asked most often:

Why do I exist? Why must I die one day? Will we be raised one day? How could man come into being? How did life begin on earth? What happens before birth? Why are people, even Christians, afraid of death? How did God come into being? Does God command us? Why are Jesus and God invisible? How is Jesus? What is the difference between Protestants, Catholics and Orthodox? What is the difference between a Christian and a Catholic? Why are there saints? What is a Moslem? What is the Koran?

That is material that can be used. But the child is demanding. He is not content with superficial and stereotyped responses. I'm thinking of the question 'Why are people, even Christians, afraid of death?' The child wants to be taken seriously and respected for who he is, not in conformity to an image which people have of him. Education must cease to be, as George Bernard Shaw put it, 'the organized defence of grown-ups against children'.

The child is an 'insurgent', wrote Simone de Beauvoir. That seems to be increasingly true. There are plenty of children who rebel silently and individually against their family and the values which it embodies. Not only our explicit values, 'work and family', but also our more or less hidden motivations, possessions, power, prestige. They not only confront us with our hypocrisy, but they make nonsense of our liking for comfort and respectability and turn towards values which seem to us to be senseless. In fact these values represent the desire that children and adolescents have for rediscovering real communication, a community life, manual work and crafts which will protect them from the consumer rat-race, from this competition and this aggressive education of which anxiety and isolation are the chief consequences.

Here is a conversation which I had with a very distinguished Jesuit who has the ear of numerous people in middle-class France.

'Doctor, are you interested in the education which has been given by the Jesuits? We have had three hundred and fifty-two colleges, and many schools are now on the premises of old Jesuit colleges.'

'As producers of the Christian neurosis, yes. You have had a particular élitist sense. I think that you have been among the worst colonizers of childhood and adolescents.'

'Colonizers? That term seems to me somewhat exaggerated.'

'Do you think so? You have had two essential aims: recruiting Jesuits and preparing the élite who will hold positions of responsibility, inexorably eliminating problem children. You have never prepared young people to change social structures and to live in a world in which men will no longer be enslaved. I know the problem very well from having seen it close to in medicine. The sole aim of the Jesuits who direct the Laënnec conference is to select future hospital doctors, future teachers and future Jesuits. I would be curious to know how many of them have remained militant Christians and what their success has been as individuals and with families. The only one of my generation who became a Jesuit has had a complete breakdown and I hope that psychiatry will get him out of it. He was a remarkably intelligent boy. Unfortunately he came to realize far too late that he had been colonized and used, and that he was psychologically under-developed. Perhaps he also had the impression of having been taken for a ride and that advantage had been taken of his juvenile enthusiasm.'

'It seems to me that your opinion is based on a limited number of cases.'

'Unfortunately that is not so. I know some Jesuit colleges which still continue to practise the same policy: their examination results are impressive, but each year there is a slaughter in the lower classes. It's a good thing that schools take people who only have average results. Your educational system perpetuates the *status quo*, that is, the identification of what you call the élite with academic results obtained after the sixth year. It's clearly a method of selection like any other. But I'm not very clear about your educative role in the Christian sense of the term. Of all my medical colleagues brought up by you, I do not know one who has remained a practising Catholic.'

'I do.'

'It's a good thing that there are some.'

'Why do you accuse the Jesuits of having encouraged the "Christian neurosis"?'

'Because of your idea of an élite and your method of selection. I often recall a brilliant boy, now a school teacher, who told me twenty-five years ago: "The Jesuits are a real scream. They push someone like me who is a real Protestant." Human growth and development have never been your objectives. It's not enough to have an important title to have a superego, and you've contributed towards producing numerous educated élites whom you continue to advise.'

'Doctor, I can see that you don't like the Jesuits.'

'Don't be mistaken; I think them remarkable, provided that they are not involved in education.'

At the eleventh congress of former pupils of the Jesuit Fathers which met at Vannes between 27 and 30 August 1975, some complained of 'excessive constraints in training once experienced in the colleges and the danger of a mechanical attitude towards the faith and Christian life'. It was even said that the colleges did not open up young people adequately to social and political life, and the life of the church with all its changes. The conservative and paternalistic approach of the President of the Federation did not pass unnoticed. In his opening address, he said: 'Faith is not an indefinite search. It has a very precise content. We should hope that our children are not contaminated by the errors which find their way into study of the catechism on the pretext of respecting liberty. In the proposal that there should be a delay in the administration of baptism there is a renewal of man's tendency to pride and a refusal to acknowledge original sin. In the logic of this reasoning there is a denial of redemption and the divinity of Jesus Christ.'

The man with whom I had been talking was silent for a few moments. He seemed caught up in some private dream. Then he said, 'How would you go about "decolonizing" the child?'

'By having as a goal the fulfilment of children, and a homogeneous psychological and intellectual development: one of the characteristics of the Christian neurosis is this division between a good intellectual quotient, even an excellent one, and an infantile psychological quotient. Many Christians are content with a certain number of reassuring gestures: going to mass, making their confession two or three times a year, paying their contribution towards the clergy, putting money in the collection, and giving money for handicapped children or black babies, the victims of drought.'

'All the same, don't these gestures have a certain value?'

'Obviously, but they're not enough. In the last resort they are ways of avoiding guilt. If all the élites formed by the Jesuits were real Christians, they would not give the left wing a monopoly in opposition. I cannot see a better form of opposition than to educate young people to allow them to accept the changes which we feel to be indispensable. In the *Revue de Sociopsychanalyse*, the psychoanalyst Gérard Mendel and his team estimate that the child is an exploited class, like women and immigrants: the disintegration of the social consensus founded on authority is such that there are only two possible consequences: either the institution of a police state charged with indoctrinating the young, or the institutionalization of the conflicts between children and adults. As an indication of this conflict, let me mention what happened in April 1972 in Dortmund: a pastor included in his parish newsletter an appeal to the children of his area to protest against the lack of playground space. This appeal was couched as a pastiche of the *Communist Manifesto*: "Children of the world, unite." The children were enthusiastic, but the parents unleashed such a storm of protest that the church authorities felt obliged to reprimand the pastor for incitement to rebellion.'

'I'm not very clear about your proposed solution.'

'I suggest that adults, the social superego, the hierarchical superego of the church, should listen to the world of children and adolescents to be able to respond to its needs. For example, if we remove from the "children's mass" its traditional character of preparation for the sacrament, to allow children to express their faith in their own way, we risk coming up against gestures and formulations which match neither our doctrine nor our customs. What is certain is that we can allow two key ideas to be put to us. One comes from Sigmund Freud, the founder of psychoanalysis. "Think of the sorry contrast between the burgeoning intelligence of a child and the mental feebleness of the average adult." The other comes from the founder of Christianity, Jesus of Nazareth: "Whoever does not receive the kingdom of God as a little child will not enter into it." The only way of "decolonizing" the child is perhaps to begin together, adults and children, on the way to discover new territory unknown to us. We can no longer allow ourselves to ignore children's poetry under the pretext that it is written in bad French or English.'

11

Worker Priests

The church has missed its way with the working world. The views of Cardinal Daniélou are interesting in this respect. 'I think that if we want to understand the feeling of many priests, we must realize that they regard it as part of the church's original sin that in the nineteenth century it failed to make contact with the working-class world. There, in their view, is a blot which must be removed at any cost. Hence there is often a kind of over-bid in this direction; they have a bias towards the workers and a perpetual desire to dissociate themselves from the middle class.' Later on, Cardinal Daniélou accused the de-Christianized middle classes of having failed also. Unfortunately, the church has failed in another point of contact, that of the Mission de France, charged with training worker priests.

I was personally involved in this experiment, as a medical psychologist, when the Mission de France had been removed to the seminary of Pontigny, in the Yonne. The seminary was in Limoges before moving to Pontigny. In the evening the seminarians went out to talk with the workers in the cafes or to go dancing. They were obsessed with the need to have contacts with the working-class world, and had a systematically anti-middle-class approach; everything was middle-class: culture, music, painting and so on. Here we find once again the idea of 'workerism' of which Cardinal Daniélou spoke.

In fact the great problem is that the church has not really thought about what should be the training, the selection and the involvement of priests in the working world. As always, when there is a problem to be resolved, it creates an institution or a committee or a sub-committee, and in so doing believes that work can go forward without any problems. In the particular case of the Mission de France, there had been no thought before the institution was created. Selection was nil. The seminary brought together a certain number of young men, anxious, unstable, some even with character problems. One of them was in his fourth seminary. This house should have been a training school, selecting young priests who had already had some experience. In fact, for some of them it became a refuge. The teaching also left a great deal to be desired. It was necessary to link classical theological training with social, economic, political and professional training. It is a pity that the church did not take as much trouble over the training of the worker priests as it did with the Jesuits. The working world has need of very mature, very cultured and professionally valuable priests. Too many of them have been overcome by their first contact with militant trade unionists and very well-trained Marxists. The school of the Party is better organized than the church.

The training of worker priests was sabotaged by lack of reflection. Once again, the neurotic institution did not communicate with itself, to understand the needs of the ego represented by the working world, a demanding and realistic ego. The distant and rigid superego thought it enough to create a seminary to respond to a vital need. The hierarchy then condemned this experiment, for which it was fully responsible.

In 1953, when the first measures were taken against the worker priests, there were about eighty diocesan priests at work, forty of them in the Paris region, along with twenty religious. Paris, Bordeaux, Toulouse, Lille, Limoges, Lyons and Marseilles were the chief centres of the Mission. The interventions made by the Curia were gradual, because the French bishops were in favour of continuing the experiment. The five conditions authorizing the work of worker priests were made known on 15 September 1953. Two of them seemed unacceptable: the limitation of the work to three hours a day and the ban against taking a temporary job. The worker priests publicized these conditions and denounced the archbishops and the political aftermath of their decision. Some of them, with the connivance of their bishop, moved on, thus affirming for the first time that a believer cannot be constrained to act against his conscience when he is pursuing a legitimate end.

Georges Houdin, a Catholic journalist, was a staunch defender of the cause of the worker priests. In an article entitled 'The traditional church knocked off its feet by the worker priest experiment', published in *Les Informations Catholiques Internationales* of October 1973, he writes,

At that time I was corresponding every week with Vladimir d'Ormesson, who was ambassador to the Vatican. An intelligent Christian, he was not content with representing the French state to the Roman authorities. He was the ambassador of all the Christians in France. It was obvious that the authorities in the Curia did not speak our language. Our friendly disposition towards the worker priests was notorious. Even our journals were suspect. Vladimir d'Ormesson, who had a sense of humour when he was writing a letter, not to mention feelings of friendship, wrote to reassure me. 'This week I was obliged to visit all the offices of the Curia. I took the opportunity to speak of your affairs. People don't have a bad opinion of you, they're even delighted at the modern character that you've managed to give your publications. In conclusion, I think that I can affirm that as long as your print-run is high and your success certain, you have nothing to fear at the Vatican.' That was a big lesson for me. It was permissible to show some independent thought as long as one succeeded financially. Poor worker priests! They were neither well-disposed nor rich. They had difficulties with the bosses and with the police. Two of them had been arrested during a demonstration against General Ridgway. Why should they be tolerated?

Of the seminarians I knew at Pontigny, some still come to consult me: one is a farm worker. His priestly activity is limited to saying mass on Sunday in the three country parishes in his charge. Another is a taxi driver. He can be free on Thursday to teach the catechism. The majority of them have stayed in a team and work in a certain number of working-class parishes. I know some good people among them who would have made excellent worker priests and would have borne powerful witness in a world ready to welcome and accept them. . . All of them regret the abortive experiment. One day the church should respond to this need: priests trained to be involved professionally and socially at the grass roots.

Another very closely related problem seems important: many young priests suffer from not being able to have a job. They are incapable of earning their living and feel that they are shut up in a situation without any alternative. Two cases have struck me particularly. These two priests questioned their vocation, one at forty and the other at forty-four; one left for Canada where he married and now has a job, the other killed himself. I am persuaded that if they had been able to realize themselves in an activity which satisfied them, the problem would have been different. They were both obsessed by the need to earn their living, to be men among other men. They needed to prove to themselves that they were like other people. I quote these two cases because the cause of the depression was the same.

The first reacted quickly. First he tried to work as a manual worker (washing up and sweeping) in the winter resort where he was priest. Soon exhausted by this ambigous situation, he had the courage to take a firm decision. He asked his bishop for 'reduction to the lay state', obtained it and left France. He went to Canada, where he married a former religious whom he had known some years before. He undertook studies which allowed him to work as a marriage counsellor. I received the news of his first child. The photograph which came with his letter was that of a happy family. The second man was very immature, intelligent and cultured. He suffered from having no sexual life and no job. He began to undergo psycho-therapy, and then gave it up. His first emotional and sexual experi-ence ended in failure. He hesitated a long time to ask to be laicized, because he was afraid of throwing himself into the working world without a diploma and with no qualifications.

On the one hand, traditional training at a major seminary does not make professional retraining easy. On the other hand, the work of the priest is still much valued. It puts those involved in it on an equal footing with all Christians, no matter what their cultural and professional level – indeed it even puts them on a superior level, as representatives of Christ.

This priest was caught between two fires. He wanted to marry, but did not want children because he was afraid of the responsibility of being the head of a family. He wanted to stop being a priest, yet he wanted to retain the authority and the prerogatives which were attached to this function. In short, he was at an impasse. After hesitating for several months, he met his bishop and officially put forward his request to be laicized. All his friends were relieved; they had the feeling that he had come out of his depression. Two days later he committed suicide in the night, by a mixture of gas and drugs.

This priest could not choose. It is true that his lack of maturity was the reason for his hesitations. He was incapable of abandoning his personage. I had been wrong in not being more directive, at least for the moment. I thought that time was on his side. In fact, while seeming to remain on balance, deep down he was deteriorating. Anxiety threatened him; the death-impulse won.

The commitment required of priests who are ordained young is a serious one. Who can be certain whether they will bear celibacy and solitude all their lives? It is impossible to deny the pathological and psychological crises which any individual can undergo. Many priests find solitude difficult to take: an emotional crisis in the forties is frequent. They discover late not only the importance of relationships with women, but also the difficulty of living without a human family and without children. When I see a priest in a crisis I often advise that he should take a job, to allow himself a breathing space and time for relaxation. However, taking a job poses problems: full-time work does not allow an individual to assume his responsibility as a priest, and part-time work gives him a particular stamp which does not allow him to find an interesting job.

What is the solution? 135 French bishops met at Lourdes for the annual Bishops' Conference, and had as a priority on their agenda the preparation for the priestly ministry. They revealed dramatic figures: between 1963 and 1971 the total number of seminarians dropped from 21,713 to 8,391. Over the same period the number of ordinations fell from 573 to 237. Ten French dioceses did not provide a single seminarian last year. The man behind the study is Monsignor François Fretellière, a man of forty-seven, from the Sulpicians. Monsignor Fretellière thinks that there are 'very open-hearted' young people whom the term 'seminarian' dissuades.

In the fight against the Christian neurosis, it is important that the ghetto seminaries should disappear. The internal reform which has been carried out does not seem to be enough. As one superior said, 'The seminarians risk dying cured'. Two new experiments are being tried. Sixty-nine candidates for the priesthood are at present being trained on the job, in a working-class context. Among the students, groups with university training are directing 133 future priests. These figures, though still modest, are likely to increase at the expense of classical seminaries. In the latter, the classes are becoming smaller and smaller.

There are ninety-eight dioceses in France, each one of which was once proud of having its own major seminary. Now there are only forty seminaries. The candidate for the priesthood can choose from among them, and no longer necessarily goes to the region where he was born. In Econe, in Switzerland, there is even a traditionalist seminary, where Latin and the soutane are still the order of the day.

In the church in France, there are numerous indications of a concern for research and reform. At Lourdes, the bishops did not wear their episcopal robes, and dressed entirely in grey or black.

It seems that the historic separation between the clergy, who had all the responsibility, and the faithful, who had very little, is now definitely a thing of the past. In future, the clergy will increasingly be replaced by the laity. Already, teaching the catechism, administering the property of the church and the direction of Catholic Action are in the hands of volunteer lay workers. Mgr Fretellière suggests that some lay people should be admitted to courses at the seminary: 'They would benefit from the courses of gifted teachers who have no pupils.'

One experiment which seems to me to be even more interesting was made by the then Anglican Bishop of Stepney, in charge of working-class suburbs in the East End of London. His area contains ninety-eight parishes with a preponderance of working-class population. There are very few priests who were born and brought up in the area where they work. 'The failure of the church in this part of London,' explained Dr Huddleston, 'is that it is not indigenous. Hitherto we have put our best and most dedicated clergy here, but the church has not progressed because its priests come from elsewhere.' That is why in 1969 he decided to appeal to the local communities themselves. At Whitsuntide, the bishop organized a referendum in all the parishes of the diocese, to put to them the idea of an indigenous auxiliary clergy and to call for volunteers. The idea was taken up enthusiastically, and six men volunteered, with the agreement and the active support of their wives and the parish which approved of their candidature. For various reasons, two of the candidates had to drop out, but the other four were ordained deacon in December 1972. They continued to work towards the priesthood, and were ordained in 1974. These men were a shop-keeper (aged 61), a telephone engineer (aged 40), a mechanic (aged 26) and a roofer (aged 32). Only the third of these was born a Christian; the others were converted. Their study for the priesthood, spread out over five years, included a theoretical part (reading theological books, an evening course with their parish priest, meetings and discussions) and a practical part (joining in the liturgical and community life of the parish and being trained in the pastoral tasks of the clergy). This preparation for the ministry proved to be very hard work because it took place outside working hours, and each of the priests was married. It was not always easy for the four of them to be free at the same time, and most of the hours of training were at the expense of family life. However, wives and children showed a good deal of understanding. To symbolize this family solidarity, the day the men were ordained to the diaconate the wife of each ordinand knelt beside her husband in front of the bishop.

There is another important innovation: this new ministry is localized in time and space, since the four future priests committed themselves to exercise their ministry for a period of seven years and in a given parish. At the end of this period they can renew their engagement with the agreement of the bishop and the Christian community which they serve. This system should allow considerable flexibility and give each one the possibility of fulfilling well-determined tasks.

Dr Huddleston affirmed:

I do not want to question the sacramental and permanent character of the priesthood. This new experiment simply sets out to be one of the possible ways of getting over the present crisis. . . We think that the sacred ministry is open to everyone, and not just to the universities. Furthermore, in my view the priesthood is not a personal charisma. The ministry must be supported by a community. Of course, we, too, hope to develop new forms of lay ministry, but in the church, priests will always be needed, and if possible, priests who also represent as perfectly as possible the Christian communities which they have come from and to which they devote themselves.

I am sorry that Père Perrin is no longer here to see this kind of development. After Rome's condemnation of the worker priest, he left his factory at Isère-Arc. He was doubtful about the future and wrote the letter in which he asked for laicization. He did not send it. Some time later he was killed in a motor-cycle accident. In 1945 he had written a book entitled *Worker Priest in Germany*. He had left in 1943 with the 700,000 young people required by the Nazi occupying force. In this book he spoke of the complete indifference of the French workers to the truths of the faith as presented to them, the coherence of their human group, and the new nature of their hopes. He prophesied what should be tomorrow's church, with a new clergy and militants mixed in with other men, sharing their work and their struggles for justice.

The clerical hierarchy has at last realized that it can no longer be content to preach patience and submission to the working-class world, and that the problem is to make the word of God understandable to people who no longer understand it. Must it not also cease to be content with prescriptions, and involve itself deeply in this development? Will the neurotic institution agree to dying to itself?

12

Epilogue: Jesus, Free Man

Christian education is in perpetual conflict with the message of the gospel, and it is based on a serious contradiction.

At a very early stage the child to whom one speaks of love and giving himself is subjected to a series of prohibitions and taboos, and told that if he goes wrong he puts himself in a state of sin. He is prevented from discovering pleasure and joy. All pleasure is sin. Sexual pleasure is clearly the prime sin, all the more in that educators, priests, religious, old women or good traditionalist Christians are deprived of it. Some project their obsessive frustration on the children whom they bring up or, more precisely, whom they make to feel guilty.

Freud defined libido as the energy derived from sexual drives. In Jung, the notion of libido is expanded to the point of denoting the 'psychical energy' generally present in everything that is a 'tendency towards'. In denying the importance of the sexual drive, its development and its realization, Christian education creates an inhibition of psychological energy, mental tone and the pleasure of living in general.

Think of the number of castrated Christians which this has produced, who, caught between desire and defence, live in fear of everything! Phobic, anxious, sometimes physically ill or impotent, they lead their petty lives, psychologically cramped, day to day in all good conscience constructing their eternal salvation.

As an adult, the Christian is faced with a permanent contradiction: he must live out a word of love in a world where only patrimony, money and inheritance are respected by all, including the majority of priests and the clerical hierarchy.

The Christian must identify himself with Jesus Christ, who was the very type of the free man, challenging all the structures of his time. In fact, Jesus relativized the law. His teaching brought about a profound change in relations between people and the institution constructed by this law and charged with its observance: he redefined the way which leads to God, the love of one's neighbour and not legalism. He shifted the centre of gravity in religion and rendered useless any institution organized for the defence and maintenance of the law. That was the real cause of his execution.

The law came from Moses, or at least was validated by his authority. By making an alliance with the Jewish people, God had imposed this law on them as a sign of their allegiance, as a witness of their fidelity. In return, he guaranteed them eternal life and blessedness. Suddenly, in this well-structured world, a man from Galilee called Jesus put forward subversive views. He transgressed the power of the scribes and Pharisees by denying the basis of their authority. He was at ease with the ne'er-do-wells, and kept company with people who had a bad reputation, who had no place in a society controlled by the 'perfect' and the priestly caste. He proved to be free from social prejudice and mixed with tax-collectors of doubtful reputation, who were regarded as thieves. He allowed prostitutes to kiss his feet. He went even further: he even ventured to claim that tax-collectors and prostitutes would precede the supercilious guardians of the law into the kingdom of heaven. He was no less free towards political power, and refused to engage in calculations and compromises. He would not allow the Zealots, the resistance movement struggling against Roman power, to use his personal ascendancy to serve the cause of national liberation. Paradoxically, it was as a result of being charged with political rebellion that he was condemned by the Romans.

Jesus always struggled against rites and against the neurotic observance of the law. He denounced legal stupidity and niggardliness: when people censured him for having cured on the sabbath day, he replied: 'Which of you, if he has a sheep fallen into a pit on the sabbath day, will not go to get it out?' His whole attitude was based on a single law: his effective love of his neighbour. He does not constrict himself by adding up transgressions of the law. For him the faith of the paralysed man or the love of the sinful woman proves that they are near to God: they have understood the meaning of 'the kingdom of God'.

There was nothing of the ascetic aiming for perfection in Jesus. 'With whom shall I compare this generation?' he said. 'It is like children sitting in the market place saying, "We have played the flute and you have not danced, we have intoned a funeral chant and you have not beaten your breasts." John (the Baptist) came neither eating nor drinking, and people said, "He's gone mad." The Son of Man (Jesus) came both eating and drinking, and people said, "Behold a glutton and a drunkard, a friend of tax-collectors and sinners." '

Jesus did not follow the way of John the Baptist. He did not retire into the desert to live a life of fasting and asceticism. He stayed among people, making contact with all social classes, both the religious professionals and those of doubtful morality. He did not think it beneath him to join in a wedding or to drink wine. He lived with a freedom which no god-fearing man dared allow. His attitude threatened the social and religious equilibrium of the Judaism of the first century. His authority and his liberty explain conflicts which, provoked by what he said, finally led to his condemnation.

His message was that of the anti-neurotic: faced with a rigid society, legalistic and mistrusting, he showed that only communication, love and respect for people, no matter whom, led to God. His message was not that of fear, anxiety or guilt. It was that of a free man, accepting no compromise and preferring to transgress rather than to obey a coercive and infantilizing law. It is incomprehensible that such a message could have given birth to a neurotic church with an attitude of perpetual compromise.

People have said that Christianity was a revolution which was never born. The church always has been and remains the institution most capable of thwarting all revolutions. It has been rapidly integrated into patrimonial society, based on the family, property and inheritance. It became a hierarchical institution, with its own structures and its temporal interests to defend. Even worse, however, it completely changed the meaning of its initial message. It established a morality founded not on love but on fear of death and the last judgment. It based its education on the crucifixion and not on the resurrection: Christ was crucified because of his love and his liberal behaviour, all qualities which do not accord well with the needs of a church and an organization. But he was raised and by the same token acknowledged to be Son of God.

Crucifixion and resurrection: the real problem lies there. The death to self favoured by Christian morality is not submission to the other person; it is not submission to a legalistic superego inculcating feelings of guilt. Its meaning is quite different: to die to oneself is to lose the primitive narcissism which makes someone incapable of any real social life and any deep relationship with others. It is to pass from being an object, subject to prohibitions and taboos, to being a responsible, autonomous subject, capable of loving oneself and others deeply. There, it seems to me, is the real sense of resurrection which makes us free men, sons of God.

The neurotic interpretation made by the church and the oppressive education to which that leads is the reason why so many Christians, priests and religious, remain fragile and anxious. They are in a state of perpetual destruction and reconstruction, never completing dying in order to live. One of them said to me, 'According to what the priests say, I'm made up of all kinds of pieces: I am a prefabricated being.'

I hope that the hierarchy of the church will rediscover a true and liberating language, and develop an education which will allow the people of our time to be healthy in body and spirit. 'I say to you: Love your neighbour as yourself and you will escape from your paralysis, your selfishness and your fear. You will no longer be a childish and anxious being, but a free man, son of Man and son of God.'

NOTES

1. The Oedipus complex is the organized group of loving and hostile desires which the child shows towards its parents. In its so-called positive form, the complex appears as in the story of King Oedipus: a desire for the death of the rival who is a figure of the same sex, and sexual desire for the figure of the opposite sex. In its negative form it presents itself the other way round: love for the parent of the same sex and jealous hate of the parent of the opposite sex. In fact these two forms can be found in differing degrees in the so-called complete form of the Oedipus complex.

The Oedipus complex plays a fundamental role in the structuring of the personality and the orientation of human desire. One can in fact detect a whole series of mixed instances, between the positive and the negative form, in which these two forms coexist in a dialectical relationship. Here the analyst has to determine the different positions adopted by the subject in the assumption and resolution of his Oedipus complex.

2. The ego is an authority which Freud, in his second theory of the organization of the psyche, distinguishes from the id and the superego.

3. The ego presents itself as a mediator, charged with the interests of the whole person, but its autonomy is only relative. It is dependent on the demands of the id (see p. 59), the imperatives of the superego and the requirements of reality. The superego is formed by the internalization of the demands of circumstances and parental prohibitions: its role is comparable to that of a judge or a censor of the ego. Freud sees the functions of the superego as being in the moral conscience, observation of the self and the formation of ideas.

4. Autogenous Schultz training is a method which teaches the subject to relax mentally and to control his emotional reactions and their psychological repercussions.

5. The major religious communities, above all the convents, are now giving considerable liberty to their members, who may therefore live the life of lay people. This tendency is becoming increasingly marked. For many religious this change of life could be an exciting development if they were prepared for it.

6. On a psychological level the castration complex is centred on the fantasy which gives the child an answer to the enigma posed to him by the anatomical difference between the sexes. He attributes this difference to the fact that the penis of a girl has been cut off. The structure and the consequence of the castration complex are different in boys and girls. Boys feel castration as the realization of a threat made by their father in response

to their sexual activities: this results in an intense 'castration anxiety'. Girls feel the absence of the penis as a loss which they seek to deny, compensate for, or remedy. The castration complex is closely connected with the Oedipus complex and more particularly with the latter's prohibitive or normative function.

7. *Pour un nouveau médecin de famille*, 1970 and *Vivre sa guérison*, 1972, both Editions Flammarion, Paris.

8. A psychologist and doctor, formerly Rector of the Faculty of Madrid, who won an international reputation for his works.

9. Transcription of an address given at a general audience on Wednesday 8 August 1973.

DATE DUE